CW00658913

The Wiccan
Almanac

The Wiccan Almanac

A Year of Magic and Tradition

SARAH BARTLETT

PIATKUS

PIATKUS

First published in Great Britain in 2024 by Piatkus

1 3 5 7 9 10 8 6 4 2

A CIP catalogue record for this book
is available from the British Library.

ISBN 978-034943-980-8

Typeset in Minion by M Rules
Printed and bound in Great Britain by
Clays Ltd, Elcograf S.p.A.

Papers used by Piatkus are from well-managed forests
and other responsible sources.

Piatkus
An imprint of
Little, Brown Book Group
Carmelite House
50 Victoria Embankment
London EC4Y 0DZ

An Hachette UK Company
www.hachette.co.uk

To all who follow the Wiccan way.
Blessings be.

CONTENTS

AUTHOR'S NOTE

'You are a child of the universe no less than the
trees and the stars; you have a right to be here.
And whether or not it is clear to you, no doubt the
universe is unfolding as it should.'

MAX EHRMANN,
Desiderata

This mystical almanac revolves around the Wiccan Wheel of the Year. It will teach you how to engage with the power of traditional Wiccan practices and festivities so that you can reconnect to the magic of the seasons, your own sacred nature and the divine.

The Wheel of the Year celebrates nature's changing energy through the seasons, and showcases eight Wiccan festivals and twelve full-moon phases over a twelve-month period. It is a beautiful pathway by which to connect with nature's cycles, bringing not only peaceful and loving influences into your life, but also vibrancy, celebration and joy.

By aligning with the magic of the never-ending cycle of seasonal change, you will feel balanced, nurtured and self-empowered, and it can allow you to discover a more authentic and natural way of living. As you dance in time with nature's rhythm, *The Wiccan Almanac* will encourage you to nourish your soul and deepen your experience of being at one with the universe.

INTRODUCTION: WICCA

'O most honored Greening Force, You who roots in the Sun;
You who lights up, in shining serenity, within a wheel
that earthly excellence fails to comprehend.
You are enfolded
in the weaving of divine mysteries.
You redden like the dawn
and you burn: flame of the Sun.'

HILDEGARD VON BINGEN,
Causae et Curae

THE ORIGINS OF WICCA

In 1921, the British archaeologist, folklorist and anthropologist Margaret Murray published *The Witch Cult in Western Europe*, in which she suggested that an ancient pagan religion based on witchcraft rituals was still secretly practised across Europe. To support her theory, Murray referenced testimony from several witch trials, but the majority of twentieth-century historians and thinkers felt that Murray's assertions lacked concrete evidence. However, some of her peers shared her beliefs, including the British occultist Gerald Gardner, who is today considered by most neopagan communities to be the 'father of Wicca'. According to most accounts, Gardner had been intrigued by the esoteric, magic and paganism for many years, and was fascinated by all forms of occultism.

At the end of the nineteenth century, the occult British group known as the Hermetic Order of the Golden Dawn (one of its founders, A. E. Waite, developed the Rider–Waite–Smith Tarot deck) had revived Hermetic esotericism, as Europe enjoyed a renaissance in occult magic and spirituality. One of the order's members was the notorious occultist Aleister Crowley. A controversial figure, Crowley had a huge influence on twentieth-century Western magic and Tarot, and developed his own spiritual belief system, which was known as 'Thelema'. The core of Thelemic thought can be distilled into 'Do as thou wilt', and the practice included ceremonial sex and what Crowley referred to as drug-induced 'magick' for initiates.

A key tenet of the Wiccan Rede (considered the Wiccan ethical code) states: 'An ye harm none, do what ye will.' There are echoes here of Crowley's belief that we should be able to do as we wish, but with the added caveat that your actions should not harm yourself or others. Gardner was influenced by Crowley's work, as well as a wide range of esoteric literature, including the occultist Dion Fortune's books on ritual magic, the folklorist Charles G. Leland's pagan classic *Aradia: Gospel of the Witches*, and Sir James Frazier's *The Golden Bough*, a comparative study of mythology and religion.

However, it appears that Margaret Murray's work had the greatest impact on Gardner, as it encouraged him to revive what he deemed the 'old religion'. Gardner asserted that he had discovered a worshipping coven in the New Forest in southern England, not far from his home, and that this gave credence to Murray's theory that secret covens existed. In the 1940s, intent on making sure that this ancient tradition survived, Gardner formed his own coven, the Bricket Wood Coven. The initiates were referred to as the 'the wica' (from an Anglo-Saxon word for 'wise crafters'). Although Gardner never personally used the term 'Wicca', the name took root as the number of people interested in his ideas grew exponentially. The Bricket Wood Coven evolved into Gardnerian Wicca, an initiatory mystery tradition that still keeps its practices secret, and from which there came many offshoots.

In 1953, the English author and poet Doreen Valiente was initiated into the Bricket Wood Coven, and was eventually named High Priestess. Much of Gardner's work was fragmented, and Valiente played a key role in adapting and developing his notes on ancient rites and spells into a structured framework, embellishing this with poetic rituals, such as her interpretation of the Wiccan Rede and the 'Charge of the Goddess' (a sacred text recited during traditional Wiccan ritual ceremonies). She is considered the mother of modern witchcraft, and Valiente's esoteric wisdom and inspiration have profoundly influenced the development of Wicca, and the worldwide decentralised neopagan movement that it is today.

WICCA IN PRACTICE

Wiccan practice is a way for Wiccans to give thanks to the deities, the earth and nature; to honour nature's cycles; to align to the seasons; and to celebrate the sabbats (festive breaks) and esbats (relevant lunar phases). Wiccans work with the four elements, a variety of deities (such as the Triple Goddess and the Horned God, as well as deities from other pantheons), nature's mysteries, the planets and constellations, and spirits of nature and wildlife. It is also common for Wiccans to engage in various forms of eclectic, green or white witchcraft, all with the intention of connecting to the divine and for the good of all.

THE WHEEL OF THE YEAR

The Wheel of the Year is an integral part of Wiccan practice, and acts as a sacred pathway for both self-development and personal growth by encouraging the practice of meaningful rituals to align with nature. As I've mentioned, the calendar is derived from pagan seasonal celebrations that draw on Druid, Celtic and ancient Irish traditions.

Part of Gerald Gardner's practice was driven by a desire to revive nature-based traditions, and he and Ross Nichols, who is often referred to as the father of modern Druidry, both encouraged the celebration of key seasonal dates. Nichols, a Cambridge academic, historian and poet, revived an interest in Druidry (Druids were high-ranking priests in pagan Celtic cultures, authenticated by Greek and Roman writers and historians) by emphasising the importance of Celtic mythology and including seasonal dates in ritual practice. He later went on to found the Order of Bards, Ovates and Druids in 1964. Nichols's Druids celebrated the equinoxes and solstices at first, while Gardner's Wiccans celebrated the Celtic festivals of Imbolc, Beltane, Lughnasadh and Samhain. Known as cross-quarter days, these mark the midpoints between the solstices and equinoxes. In the late 1950s, the two practices merged, giving rise to the complete Wheel of the Year that most modern pagans and Wiccans now follow.

Please note that for the purposes of this book, I am working with the northern hemisphere. For example, when I talk about the summer solstice of c. 21 June, this is the winter solstice for southern hemisphere dwellers.

Similarly, I refer to a new crescent moon as being an 'arc of light curving outwards to the right' according to the northern hemisphere, but in the southern hemisphere a new crescent moon would be seen as an arc of light curving outwards to the left.

Sabbats and esbats

The eight sabbats that make up the Wheel of the Year celebrate nature's rhythms and seasonal shifts. Aligning with these transitional dates enables us to go with the flow and to find balance and harmony in our own lives. We can then connect to nature more fully and become aware of seasonal changes and what they might mean to us.

- the winter solstice or Yule (c. 21 December)
- Imbolc (1 February)
- the spring equinox (c. 20 March)
- Beltane (1 May)
- the summer solstice (c. 21 June)
- Lughnasadh or Lammas (1 August)
- the autumn equinox (c. 21 September)
- Samhain (1 November)

The eight sabbat festivities are a chance for Wiccans to draw on empowering energy and celebrate our synergy with the natural world. They can be celebrated with rituals specific to each coven (often highly secret), or more generally with seasonal offerings, feasting and dancing to invoke the power of the Earth Goddess (the Triple Goddess) and the Sun God (the Horned God).

Esbats are celebrations of the full moon cycle (and other lunar phases, according to specific covens) throughout the year. Depending on the coven or tradition followed, the esbats usually honour and give thanks to the Triple Goddess, or a moon goddess who aligns with a specific intention or goal – especially when engaging in spell work. It is also possible to worship a particular aspect of the Triple Goddess depending on the time of the year. For example, if it is a full moon in early February, you might like to draw on the power of Brigid, who is a favoured Maiden goddess at Imbolc (1 February). We will explore the Triple Goddess in more detail below.

The solar cycle

The path of the sun through the ecliptic (its orbit around planet Earth) during the year marks the four key points of the Wheel of the Year. The two equinoxes (when night and day are of equal length) and the two solstices (the longest and shortest days of the year) form the basic framework of the Wheel, and the four other midpoints or cross-quarter days fit within this. The Wheel of the Year also offers a structure from which to understand the Wiccan myth cycle, which refers to the story of the eternal interaction between the Earth Goddess and the Sun God.

THE LUNAR CYCLE

Throughout the year, the changing energy of the moon's cycle is also celebrated. Most Wiccan witches perform spells according to the phases of the moon. In Wicca, there are three main phases of the moon's cycle associated with the Triple Goddess symbol, which identifies the moon with the Maiden (waxing moon), Mother (full moon), and Crone (waning/dark of the moon). There are Wiccans who use four phases of the moon (the waxing moon, the full moon, the waning moon and the dark of the new moon), but in this book, I will refer to the Triple Goddess cycle.

The waxing moon is creative, seductive and inspiring. It aligns with late winter and springtime, and the Maiden aspect of the Triple Goddess. This is a time to perform spells or rituals that call on the deities for new beginnings, to help you get projects off the ground, and to encourage new romance and beneficial energy.

The full moon is a time of culmination and fruition. It aligns with the summer, the first harvests of autumn, and the Mother aspect of the Triple Goddess. Use this phase of the moon to perform spells and rituals that call on the deities for empowerment and to help you fulfil goals and finalise plans.

The waning moon is a time for letting go, listening to wise counsel, reflecting and resting. This phase aligns with the Crone or Old Woman, covering both the end of autumn and the dark of winter. It can be beneficial when engaging in rituals or spells that call on the deities to help you relinquish the past, banish bad habits, or protect you from negative psychic or geopathic energy.

THE TRIPLE GODDESS AND THE HORNED GOD

Wiccans often use the Triple Goddess and Horned God symbols in their work. The Triple Goddess encompasses the various aspects of the Great Goddess, also known as the Earth Goddess, who is believed to be the archetypal mother goddess of ancient civilisations, and from whom all other goddesses emanate. The Horned God is god of the wild, sexuality, the hunt and nature, and he is derived from ancient earth gods such as the Celtic god of the forests and fertility, Cernunnos, and sun gods such as the Celtic, Lugh and Bel. The Horned God symbol is made up of a circle topped by a crescent moon resembling two horns, signifying dark and light. The Triple Goddess symbol is made up of a waxing crescent moon on the left (in the northern hemisphere, the waxing crescent moon curves outwards to the right), a circle in the middle representing the full moon, and a waning crescent moon on the right (in the northern hemisphere, the waning crescent moon appears to curve outwards to the left). As we have seen, the Triple Goddess also symbolises the Maiden, Mother and Crone aspects of the goddess archetype, and corresponds to the three Wiccan seasons: spring/summer, summer/autumn, and autumn/winter.

To avoid confusion, I refer to the Triple Goddess and the Horned God as the Earth Goddess and the Sun God respectively throughout the book, as I believe the synergy between them is easier to understand and apply to one's own lifestyle in this way, and it also offers a powerful metaphor for Earth's relationship with the sun.

MYTHOLOGY

Mythology is a key feature of Wiccan practice, as most modern-day Wiccan festivities are inspired by ancient pagan celebrations of gods and goddesses, who were considered embodiments of the seasons, crops, trees, plants, planets and stars, and were worshipped to encourage fertility and a successful harvest. Myths and legends arose around these gods and goddesses, and their sacred stories helped ancient peoples to make better sense of the world. Wicca is an all-inclusive pagan system, and finds its origins in Greek, Roman, Celtic, Gaelic and Norse mythology and lore. For example, when the Romans invaded England, the Celtic goddess Sulis merged with the Roman goddess Minerva to become Sulis Minerva. Celtic paganism, according to scholars, is derived from Proto-Indo-European paganism, and as such, many of the deities and stories from Celtic mythology are rooted in earlier pagan origins. Wicca embraces all pagan beliefs, although some pagan groups may not identify with Wicca.

DEITIES

Although many formal Wiccan branches revere specific deities, such as Dianic Wicca, where only a single divine feminine power is worshipped, most solitary Wiccans are polytheistic, and include both male and female deities in their chosen pantheon. The diversity of Wicca is such that it does not exclude the melding of mythological traditions, all of which mirror our own inner landscapes and provide us with spiritual reconnection. When you choose your pantheon or specific gods and/or goddesses, consider why they hold meaning for you and whether you resonate with their cultural origins.

You may prefer to only call on the Earth Goddess and the Sun God, or you might choose to celebrate a number of Celtic, Greek, Roman and Norse deities. All deities are aspects of the archetypal 'goddess' and 'god' figures, who both represent the divine power of the universe and reflect our own individual and collective psyche.

WITCHCRAFT

Modern Wiccan practice often involves communing with nature and giving thanks to the divine that is manifest in nature and its deities. Although witchcraft is not an essential part of the tradition, it can provide Wiccans with a practical pathway for connecting with the divine.

The type of witchcraft that you choose to practise is entirely up to you, although it is essential that your intentions are always pure and positive. You may choose to practise on your own, join an existing coven, or you might look to form your own coven with other like-minded Wiccans. There are many branches of initiate-based traditional Wiccan groups, such as Gardnerian Wicca, British Traditional Wicca and Dianic Wicca. Although these initiates keep their rituals and practices secret, ceremonial magic and calling on deities is pivotal to their practice, perhaps more so than the solitary witch's use of sympathetic, natural or folk magic.

THE FOUR ELEMENTS

The ancient Greek philosopher Empedocles (c. 494–434 BCE) was one of the first in the West to theorise that the world and everything in it was made up of four elements: fire, earth, air and water. However, it's important to note that ancient Eastern cultures had already developed their own ideas concerning these energies.

The four elements have since become the basis of many Western esoteric and pagan belief systems. There is also a fifth element, spirit (also known as 'aether', 'quintessence' or 'akasha'), described as the divine, universal or fundamental energy that connects all, or the 'spirit/soul' within oneself. One of the symbols commonly used in Wiccan witchcraft is the pentagram, a five-pointed star aligning to the five elements, with the fifth element, spirit, associated with the top point.

In Wicca, fire is a masculine principle and aligns with

the Sun God, while earth is a feminine principle and relates to the Earth Goddess. Water is feminine and relates to the moon and lunar goddesses, and air is masculine and relates to the planets, the stars, the wind and the sky. The four elements are often mentioned at the start of a ritual or spell, and are associated with the four compass directions (fire with south, water with west, earth with north and air with east). For example, the practitioner often casts a circle of protection around themselves, calling on the four directions (see page 114).

By using this symbolic system, we can deepen our wisdom, generate our intentions, and help to manifest our goals. (See the glossary for more detail on the elements.)

WICCA AND TAROT

Although the Tarot is a mystic tradition in its own right, most Wiccans who practise witchcraft or magic have a deck of these divinatory cards among their tools, just as they will have a collection of crystals, a range of herbs and candles, and a Book of Shadows (see glossary). The Tarot is aligned with the four elements and its correspondences, so in magic you can use the symbolic imagery of the Tarot to amplify or enhance your intention.

SACRED SPACE OR ALTAR

If you don't already have an altar or sacred space dedicated to Wicca or any other type of pagan belief, then this is the time to start one. It can be in any room of your choosing – you can even set one up outdoors, if you have the space – but you will need a flat surface to work on. This will be your special place to petition the deities, call on spirits, cast spells, perform rituals and place offerings and votives.

Throughout the book, you'll notice that I often suggest performing rituals on your altar, but that doesn't mean that you are limited to a specific corner of your home. It's more important to go with how you feel. Your connection to a place can change from day to day, so let yourself be guided by your intuition.

BOOK OF SHADOWS

Wiccans who practise witchcraft usually keep a Book of Shadows, which contains details of spells, ingredients and secret incantations. When Gerald Gardner first revived the witchcraft movement, he proposed that each coven should maintain their own exclusive Book of Shadows that would not be shared with outsiders. However, since the 1970s, it has become standard practice for individual witches to keep a personal Book of Shadows, whether they practise alone or with others.

Why not keep a journal filled with notes, observations, spells, herbs and rituals throughout the year as your own Book of Shadows?

HOW TO USE THIS BOOK

The start of the Wiccan Wheel of the Year varies depending on which Wiccan custom is observed. There is no definitive start or end to the cycle.

The traditional Celtic view is that the agricultural year begins at Samhain (end of harvest, 31 October/1 November), and this has been adopted by many as the start of the Wiccan year. Another popular interpretation of the Wiccan calendar, which I personally follow, mirrors the developing relationship between the Sun God and Earth Goddess, starting with the winter solstice/Yule and the rebirth of the Sun God. However, I have placed Imbolc (1 February) at the start of this book, because it feels appropriate to begin by offering a positive sense of spring in the air and the Sun God's increasing power.

With that said, it doesn't matter if it's not February when you first open this book; it is designed so that you can start at any appropriate month, and then work your way through from there.

ABOUT THE CHAPTERS

Every chapter will explore the season and any key festivals or themes associated with the month, as well as relevant folklore, the full moon, visible constellations and stars, and a key Tarot card, along with appropriate rituals or spells connected to these. All rituals and spells will draw on nature's sacred gifts corresponding to the month.

THE MONTH AT A GLANCE

Each chapter opens with a list of key qualities relating to the month in question.

SEASON AND CYCLE

We'll begin by exploring the season in which each month falls, what we can expect from the natural world at this time, and how this can affect us.

CELEBRATING

We'll move on to any pagan festivals or themes associated with the month, with a detailed exploration of whichever festival or theme is key for the month, and a series of rituals and practices that align with this theme or festival so that you can personally engage with the tradition.

Each month we will explore a specific myth, tale, god or goddess relevant to the month, and what this means for you.

WICCAN MYTH CYCLE

In this section, you can see how the synergy between the Sun God and the Earth Goddess evolves and relates to the seasons throughout the year. This is one of the simplest ways to follow the turning of the Wheel of the Year. As mentioned, the god and goddess come with different epithets or identities: the Earth Goddess encompasses both the Cailleach of Winter and Brigid, the goddess of summer, while the Sun God encompasses both the Holly King of winter and the Oak King of summer (see page 96). However, for consistency, I will stay with the basic story of the Earth Goddess and her relationship with the Sun God throughout each cycle.

THE FULL MOON

In pagan and indigenous folklore, each full moon of the year is given a name of its own that usually identifies it with the weather, the season or the month in which it falls.

Here are the traditional full moon names (from Celtic/ British folklore) for the twelve months of the calendar year:

| JANUARY | Quiet or Wolf Moon |
| FEBRUARY | Ice or Snow Moon |

MARCH	Wind or Chaste Moon
APRIL	Seed or Growing Moon
MAY	Hare or Bright Moon
JUNE	Mead Moon
JULY	Hay or Storm Moon
AUGUST	Grain or Corn Moon
SEPTEMBER	Harvest Moon
OCTOBER	Hunter's Moon
NOVEMBER	Dark Moon
DECEMBER	Oak or Cold Moon

CONNECT TO NATURE

This section provides simple rituals and practices that will allow you to engage with seasonal energy and be at one with the natural world around you.

STARLORE

I have included the best-known and most visible constellations in the sky for each month, as they give us a deeper understanding of ancient mythology, which helps to widen our Wiccan perspective of both ourselves and the universe. Our ancestors observed the stars and the planets for both practical and spiritual wisdom. We may find that our solar system and the stars beyond provide us with more knowledge than we can imagine. Just as you look to nature to feel at one with the world around you, if you look up to the stars and constellations and engage with their stories, you will feel a deep connection with the cosmos, too.

TAROT

Finally, I have also included a Tarot card for each month that traditionally corresponds to the zodiac sign that rules the majority of the calendar month in question. You can draw this card for the month and meditate upon it, or, of course, use it as an empowering symbol in any rituals or spellwork you do that month to reinforce your seasonal connection.

SPELLS AND RITUALS

INGREDIENTS

For the rituals and spells, I have included ingredients you can easily find, or may already have in your collection if you are already familiar with Wicca. But there are no truly prescribed spells here, and you are welcome to adapt and find alternative or corresponding items depending on what is available and your local environment.

CANDLES

Please note, I often suggest using tealight candles rather than taper candles for fire safety. If you prefer, you can replace these with LED candles, or just use unlit candles. However, it's worth noting that a real 'flame' has a symbolic resonance with the element of fire, and is an important connective power in spellwork.

Finally, I want to emphasise that there are no 'must-dos' here, only signposts!

The rituals in this book are simply intended to show you the way to your own connection with the universe, to help you explore how it feels to align with different energies, and to help you acknowledge that you are part of the universe, as the universe is part of you.

So please enjoy, participate, and follow the Wiccan way whenever you feel the moment is right to engage with the sacredness of all that is around and within you.

FEBRUARY

'A small bird twitters on a leafless spray,
Across the snow-waste breaks a gleam of gold:
What token can I give my friend to-day
But February blossoms, pure and cold?'

SARAH DOUDNEY,
'Snowdrops (Consolation)'

FEBRUARY AT A GLANCE

THEMES	purification, creative inspiration, anticipation
FESTIVAL/FOCUS	Imbolc (1 February)
DEITY	Brigid
CRYSTALS	amber/amethyst
ELEMENTS	air/water
FULL MOON	Ice/Snow Moon
TREE	alder
BIRD	great tit
PLANT	snowdrop
ZODIAC	Aquarius/Pisces
TAROT	the Moon

SEASON AND CYCLE

February is named after Februa, an ancient Roman festival of purification that was annually observed during this month. Throughout the northern hemisphere, it has traditionally been a month to celebrate the anticipation of the coming spring.

February's weather can be as unpredictable and contrary as the qualities of the zodiac sign that rule over most of the month (Aquarius). There are days when it feels as if the darkness of winter is finally over, but then we wake up to thick blankets of snow. With each passing day, the nights grow shorter and the days longer. At times there is a sense that spring is in the air, it's easy to be lulled into a false sense of security by the changeability of the weather. On 1 February, the Celtic festival of Imbolc marks this subtle change from winter to the coming spring.

Snowdrops are in bloom, butter-coloured celandines dot the verges and woodland, and you can hear blackbirds and great tits fine-tuning their songs for mating season, which will begin in March. This is a liminal, serene time: a time to look back on the past year without regret or anger, to let go of things that no longer serve you, and to look forward to sowing the seeds of your own spring.

CELEBRATING FEBRUARY

FESTIVAL: IMBOLC (1 FEBRUARY)

Imbolc marks a midpoint between the dark of the winter solstice (c. 21 December) and the spring equinox (c. 21 March). This day is like a light shining through the darkness that will inspire, bring insight and encourage new visions for the weeks ahead. 'Imbolc' is a Celtic word that literally translates as 'in the belly' or 'womb'. This is believed to refer to the first pregnant ewes of the season, and it's thought that Imbolc was originally a Celtic festival honouring the fertility goddess, Brigid (also known as Brigit or Bride), and her promise of spring.

Some sources say that Brigid is associated with the earlier Celtic fertility goddess Danu, who revitalised the earth each year in spring when fires were lit in her honour. Brigid means 'the fiery' or 'bright one', and she is both the goddess of rekindling the flame of creativity (the element of fire) and the goddess of sacred wells and springs and purification (the element of water). This, then, is a time when fires were lit, and sacred wells blessed. For the Celtic people, it signified the first signs of the 'light' of spring.

Although Imbolc is celebrated on 1 February as a 'midpoint sabbat' (also known as a cross-quarter day), astronomically, this midpoint may fall between 3 February and 6 February, depending on the year in question.

On the Hill of Tara in the Boyne Valley in Ireland (a ceremonial site for ancient Celtic kings), there lies a Neolithic passage tomb known as the Mound of the Hostages. It is over five thousand years old, and the entrance aligns with the rising sun twice a year, illuminating the chamber within. This happens during the days around Imbolc and Samhain. It appears these so-called 'cross-quarter days' were important to the Neolithic peoples, perhaps marking the changing influence of the sun around these dates, just as they marked it at the solstices and equinoxes. For later Celtic tribes, the Hill of Tara was also believed to be the home of their warrior god of light, Lugh (also associated with Lammas or Lughnasadh, the cross-quarter day of 1 August).

By the medieval period, Imbolc was absorbed into Christian practice and merged with both St Brigid's Day and Candlemas (it is still often referred to as Candlemas by some branches of Wicca). Candlemas is a day for celebrating the ritual purification of Mary, forty days after the birth of Jesus. Christian folk would bring their candles to church to be blessed, and in various parts of Britain, candles were also given as gifts or lit in honour of St Brigid (see page 30) to mark the coming of spring.

A RITUAL TO EMBRACE IMBOLC

This Imbolc ritual welcomes the return of light and warmth, and marks the beginning of a new season of growth, abundance, planting and fertility. Use this ritual to embrace this energy and give life to your own inspiration.

You will need:
a mirror
2 white tealight candles

1. Place the two white tealights in front of your propped-up mirror as a dedication to Imbolc.
2. Stand still for a minute by your altar and be aware of the stillness around you.
3. Next, close your eyes, and imagine yourself standing on a threshold, with the door to the winter palace closing behind you, and the door to a spring courtyard before you. Imagine yourself opening that door, and walking into the pure air of spring, blessed by the light and the blessings of the Earth Goddess and Sun God.
4. Open your eyes, safely light the candles and focus on the reflections of the two flames in the mirror, one to represent the winter, the other, spring.
5. Reflect on the winter palace you have left behind and blow out the corresponding candle, then reflect on the joy of the spring courtyard to come. When you intuitively sense that you are ready, blow out the second candle and you will feel connected to the essence of your own creativity, ready for the coming spring.

IMBOLC DECORATION IDEAS

Try out the following traditional decoration ideas to embellish your home with Imbolc energy:

- February is about purity, so choose white flowers, candles and decorations to instil your home with cleansing energy.

- To celebrate Brigid's festival, place an unlit white tealight candle as a centrepiece on your altar, surrounded by a ring of white stones and white crystals, such as moonstone or clear quartz. Dress these with a drop of clary sage essential oil (or a white flower essential oil) to invoke uplifting and revitalising energy. Place a circle of nineteen (Brigid's sacred number) white tealights around your circle of stones, to give thanks to the goddess's eternal flame of creativity.

- Gather a few branches of hazel catkins, early wild cherry blossom or pussy willow, and place them in a window to attract the Sun God's inspiring power.

- If you have any snowdrop bulbs in pots, place one on your altar just for the day to honour this noble flower. If you don't have snowdrops, fill a small glass bowl with water, and sprinkle over some white confetti or tiny scraps of white paper to symbolise the magical flower of February.

- If you decide to invite others to celebrate Imbolc with you, hang a wreath of alder catkins and cones on your front door, or place one on the table; if you like, you can weave pussy willow twigs and branches into the wreath too. This will encourage goodness and goodwill from and to all who enter your home.

- Welcome Brigid to your home by laying a place for her at your table, with a glass of milk, or some bread – her sacred offerings. As you do so, say a brief prayer of gratitude to Brigid for her gift of spring: 'Thank you, Brigid, for the light of spring. Blessed be.'

THE SNOWDROP

Snowdrops are symbolic of purity, and remind us of our release from Khione's icy power, and their own strength in withstanding her destructive energy. Khione was the Greek winter snow goddess, daughter of Boreas, the god of the freezing north wind. She is also identified with other winter goddesses, such as the Cailleach and Beira of Gaelic fame. Khione's influence is now slowly fading away, and although she can return with a vengeance, covering brave new shoots with a blanket of snow or running her frostbitten fingers across our fences, we know that the snowdrop is resilient, its purity bursting forth at this threshold between winter and spring.

RITUAL TO PURIFY YOUR SOUL AND YOUR HOME

In Celtic lore, Brigid was believed to bless the home and was celebrated for her healing powers. As she was the goddess of sacred springs and wells, pieces of cloth or rag (known as clooties) were often hung on trees around sacred wells, as votives for Brigid's healing blessings. If you can visit a sacred well or spring at this time of year, you too can petition

Brigid for her blessing. This simple ritual will not only help to cleanse the spirit of your home, but will also revitalise your own spirit, ready for the changing solar energy that is coming.

You will need:
30 cm (12 in) length of white ribbon
a white tealight candle

1. On the ribbon, write: 'Thank you, Brigid, for your spiritual blessing for myself and my home.' Go to your chosen site and tie your ribbon on a bush or tree, or simply lay it on the ground in a circle. Walk around the ribbon in a clockwise direction nineteen times (Brigid's sacred number) to seal your intention for Brigid's blessings.

2. When you return home, light a white tealight candle, and slowly walk around your home with the candle as if cleansing the space of all negativity. (If you are wary of using a candle, you can substitute this with pine incense, as pine is associated with Brigid.)

3. As you make your way round all rooms or areas of your home, say, 'Thank you, Brigid, for blessing my home with goodness and the coming spring. Blessed be.'

4. Let the candle burn down safely in its own time, to imbue your home with Brigid's flame.

MYTH

Brigid, also known as Bride, Brigit and Bridget, was the Celtic goddess of creativity, wisdom, sacred wells, springs and poetry, and, in earlier accounts, the moon and sun.

Irish myth tells how she was the daughter of Dagda, a powerful father god of the ancient Celtic supernatural race known as Tuatha Dé Danann. She later became associated with protection of the home when she was assimilated into Christianity as St Brigid. Her convent in Kildare was renowned for its magical associations (it is believed that it was previously the site of a sacred shrine to the goddess, Brigid). Here, flowers sprung up in her footprints, cows were always in milk, and her garden was eternally filled with spring growth. The twelfth-century historian, Gerald of Wales, wrote that nineteen nuns (originally the goddess's priestesses) took turns to keep a sacred fire burning in her honour. According to Gerald, the fire was encircled by a hedge, and any man who tried to cross it would be cursed.

Brigid's sacred animals include the serpent, wolf, cow and various birds of prey, and her motifs are the St Brigid's Cross and the Bride doll. Originally made from rushes, the St Brigid's Cross is an off-set cross woven around a central square. In pagan and Wiccan terms, it symbolises the four seasons and four elements, and was traditionally hung over doorways to protect the home. The Bride doll, meanwhile, represents feminine wisdom (see below).

Representing Brigid (and thus the Earth Goddess), this strange little corn doll was more of a fertility symbol than a playmate. The doll was dressed as a 'bride', and ceremoniously placed on the hearth of the home alongside a 'phallic wand' to symbolise the Sun God. The wand was usually a birch stick, with an acorn pushed on to the tip. The following day, if the ashes of the fire were disturbed, it was believed the gods had blessed your home with their union!

To bring love, creativity and the deities' blessings into your home, source a small corn dolly, or make a Bride doll of your own.

You will need:
a piece of fabric
needle and thread
your favourite dried herbs and/or dried lavender
a phallic symbol (maybe a long unlit candle or a stick – be
    as creative as you desire!)

1. To make the Bride doll, simply cut two basic doll shapes from the fabric. Stitch them almost together, leaving a small gap through which you can stuff the doll with your herbs or lavender. Once it's stuffed, stitch up the gap. (If you prefer, you can print or draw an image of Bride, cut it out and use it as a paper doll.)

2. On the evening before Imbolc, lay the Bride doll down beside your chosen phallic symbol in the

centre of your home (or in front of the fireplace, if you have one) and leave them there overnight.

3. This fertility ritual will help to release you from the winter blues, and re-energise your sense of purpose, empowering you with positivity for the months to come.

4. As I explained above, it was believed that if you looked into the ashes in the hearth the morning after leaving the Bride doll and the phallic Sun God symbol in place, you might see a meaningful pattern left from Brigid's visit. Even if you don't have an open fireplace, look around your home for any changes that may have occurred during the night, or any symbols or signs that could help guide you to know the future. Imbolc is a traditional time for divination.

BRIGID'S SACRED NUMBER

Brigid's sacred number, nineteen, echoes the moon's Metonic cycle of almost exactly nineteen years. This cycle (named after Meton, a fifth-century BCE Greek mathematician and astronomer) is how long it takes the moon to return to exactly the same spot in the sky, in exactly the same phase. So, for example, a full moon at twenty-five degrees of Aries on the ecliptic (the apparent path of the sun around the Earth) will only be seen in exactly the same position in the sky nineteen years later. According to ancient Greek historian Diodorus Siculus in his works of c. 60–30 BCE, the ancient Greeks believed that Apollo, in his aspect as the Sun God of the north, known as Hyperborean Apollo, visited the moon goddess's temple in Hyperborea, a fabulous realm of eternal springtime located in the far north, 'beyond the land of the Celts', once every nineteen years. This offers a mysterious link between the Metonic lunar cycle and Brigid's original identity as a moon goddess.

The Coligny Calendar is an ancient Celtic lunisolar (combining both lunar and solar phases) bronze plaque dating to the second century CE that was found in Coligny, France. This calendar uses the Metonic cycle to accurately calculate the solar year. It gives us insight into how the Celts 'viewed' the year as being split into a dark period and a light period (winter and summer). Similarly, each month was accorded a dark and a light half: the dark half from full moon to dark of the moon, the light half from new moon to full moon.

WICCAN MYTH CYCLE

The Wiccan myth cycle has no beginning or end, for it is essentially like the Wheel of the Year, an eternal turning of birth, life, death and rebirth, as suggested by the mythical synergy of the Sun God and the Earth Goddess. The time of Imbolc is when the Earth Goddess shakes off the identity of the Crone, and transforms into the Maiden. Imbolc is a time of purification, the return of light, and the first buds bursting forth from the ground. Similarly, the Earth Goddess, now purified, becomes fertile, preparing for her future union with the Sun God. Meanwhile, the reborn Sun God adolescent has been sleeping, and he now emerges from his winter hideaway among the ivy and mistletoe. He has yet to seek out and meet the Maiden, but his ardour grows daily as his solar light moves higher in the sky.

FULL MOON: SNOW/ICE MOON

In folklore and mythology, the full moon in February is associated with goddesses and spirits who embody winter, such as the Greek snow goddess Khione (see page 34), and the Queen of Winter, Beira (also known as the Gaelic Cailleach (see page 224), an ancient deity who ruled between Samhain (1 November) and Beltane (1 May). It was believed that if Beira felt her power was diminishing, she would create sudden frosts and spark heavy snowfall to prolong the winter.

In traditional Celtic folklore, this full moon is known as either the Snow Moon or the Ice Moon, reminding us that the Queen of Winter still reigns, and that we must respect her icy grip. For all our impatient longing for spring and the joys of summer, we must respect and honour winter, lest we slip on Beira's frozen pond and fall into the icy waters of her power.

SNOW MOON RITUAL

You will need:
a piece of paper and a pen
3 small clear quartz crystals or moonstones
a white tealight candle

1. On the evening of the February full moon, draw the symbol of the Triple Goddess (representing the three aspects of Maiden, Mother, Crone) on your piece of paper and place a crystal on each moon.

2. Carefully light the tealight candle, and place it behind the Triple Goddess. Focus your eyes on the flame of the candle, and then give thanks to the Queen of Winter by saying: 'This Snow Moon reminds me to give thanks to the Queen of Winter, as it symbolises the end of darkness and the birth of spring. Your power may be waning, but your light is still true.'

3. Now write down three words beneath your Triple Goddess symbol that describe what you would like to fulfil by the next full moon in March.

4. Leave the piece of paper by a window overnight so that it can draw on the full moon's energy, and then store it in a safe place, where it will act as a reminder of what you are going to achieve.

WHERE IS THE FULL MOON?

Once every nineteen years (yes, the Metonic cycle again – see above), there is no full moon in February. This is because the length of a lunar cycle (from full moon to full moon, say) is approximately twenty-nine and a half days, while February has only twenty-eight days (or twenty-nine days every four years). This means February will be without a full moon once every nineteen years. February's length also means it only ever has one full moon in the calendar month (all other calendar months have the potential to have two full moons, depending on where they fall within the lunar cycle).

CONNECT TO NATURE

It may seem that all is cold for much of February, but even as Beira throws her frosty, scornful winds across the hills and snaps her icy fingers, there is something rustling in the hedgerows. Midway through the month, great tits, dunnocks and robins begin to sing again to claim territory or attract potential mates, and celandines start appearing in the woods. Most mammals still hide away, but it is still possible to spot the odd deer or squirrel, popping out tentatively to join the mating game.

If you want to celebrate the joy of the coming spring, you can try the following ritual.

A CELEBRATION OF THE ALDER TREE

Alder trees favour moist ground and are happy to be submerged in water, so you'll often spot them growing beside streams, rivers and wetlands. In Celtic folklore, it was believed that if you placed a few alder leaves in your shoes (clogs were also made of alder wood), you would be protected from the damp weather.

For this ritual, you will need some alder catkins or cones, but please do not pick these without permission.

You will need:
a bowl of water
5 alder catkins or cones

1. Take the catkins or cones in one hand and hold them over the bowl of water. As you do so, affirm:

> 'With these [cones/catkins], the spirit of
>   spring will blossom within me.
> I thank you, alder tree, for your roots that
>   lie in water,
> your boughs that reach to the sky,
> your trunk that stands proud,
> and your fruits that are fired by the sun.
> I am now ready to engage in nature's
>   growth.'

2. Reflect on the opportunities for growth that spring will bring. You will feel a deeper connection to the wildscape and the protective power of the alder tree.

STARLORE

Every month, we may recognise the changing seasons, but we often overlook the changing skies. And if we cherish and love this planet as Wiccans, then we must respect and give thanks to the cosmos, of which our planet is a part. So this month, look to the southern and south-western skies on a clear night in mid to late February. Orion and Taurus are now prominent. If you look more closely, you will also see the bright stars of the Hyades cluster in Taurus. This cluster is made up of hundreds of stars, but four of the brightest (the ones you can see with the naked eye) form a 'V' shape that marks the bull's face and, from our 'world's eye view', appear not too far from the bright orange giant star, Aldebaran, which mark's the bull's eye.

The Hyades (rain nymphs) were the half-sisters of the Pleiades, and daughters of Atlas. Their brother, the hunter Hyas, was said to have either been killed by a serpent or gored by a wild boar, so the Hyades mourned his death and died of their weeping. Zeus took pity on them and placed them as a star cluster in Taurus. Their annual sighting from the end of January to the end of March in the northern hemisphere is usually accompanied by heavy rain, said to be the sisters' tears of grief.

To help you locate the Hyades, first find the three stars of Orion's Belt. Trace a line with your finger from the belt in a westward direction, until you come to the red-orange glow of Aldebaran, and there you will see the 'V' shape of four stars that belong to the Hyades cluster.

Contemplate on this weeping cluster, and how Imbolc and February are not just about rejoicing for the spring to come, but also relinquishing the past.

TAROT: THE MOON

As the sun moves into the water element of Pisces on around 20 February, our intuition may be heightened, and in the Tarot this is represented by the Moon. So this is a time to trust your intuition – not your imagination, as sometimes we confuse one with the other. The Moon is also a card of self-deception, so whenever you draw it, be aware that not all is at it seems. Your judgement may be unsound, or someone may be taking advantage of you. Identify your fears and tap in to your sixth sense to find the answer. Perhaps leave this card on your altar to remind you to listen to your inner voice, but be sure to know what your inner voice truly is.

MARCH

'It was one of those March days when the sun shines hot and the wind blows cold: when it is summer in the light, and winter in the shade.'

CHARLES DICKENS,
Great Expectations

MARCH AT A GLANCE

THEMES	arousal, awakening, adventure
FESTIVAL/FOCUS	spring equinox
DEITY	Pan
CRYSTALS	amethyst/red carnelian
ELEMENTS	water/fire
FULL MOON	Chaste
TREE	wild cherry
BIRD	dunnock
PLANT	daffodil
ZODIAC	Pisces/Aries
TAROT	the Emperor

SEASON AND CYCLE

The early nineteenth-century author, poet and translator Sara Coleridge (daughter of Samuel Taylor Coleridge), reminds us that: 'March brings breezes, loud and shrill, / Stirs the dancing daffodil.' And it is not just the daffodils that are stirring. March sees dormancy replaced by regrowth, with wild primroses bursting into flower and days gradually lengthening. Violets and wood anemone spread across the forest floor like carpets of stars across the dark earth, dandelions suddenly appear along verges, and daisies begin to dot the grass.

Out in the empty fields, hares chase one another in the mists of early dawn as part of a mating ritual. These magical creatures lie low, camouflaged against the earth. Great tits, blue tits, robins, blackbirds and many other birds begin to establish their territories and attract mates with their cheeps and tweets.

March is a month of rebirth and fresh starts. It marks the beginning of the astronomical year (and the older Roman new year), as the sun moves to zero degrees Aries on around 21 March to mark the spring or vernal equinox. At this point in the year, the sun is exactly above the equator, so from pole to pole, half of the earth is in shadow, and half is in light. This balance remains for only a brief moment in time, but it can act as a reminder of the importance of maintaining equilibrium in our lives. As if we are learning to walk on a tightrope, we have to constantly adjust, not only to the changing movement and vibrations of the rope beneath our feet, but to the changing energy all around us too. Once we cross that equinox tightrope walk, it is the perfect time to begin new projects, to embark on an adventure and to get creative. Remember how you rested and found serenity in the dark of winter in order to prepare you to go forth and find the courage to seek out your goals? Well, now it's time.

CELEBRATING MARCH

FESTIVAL: SPRING EQUINOX

The spring or vernal equinox is sometimes referred to as Ostara (a term coined by prominent Wiccan practitioner Aidan Kelly in the 1970s). This relates to the Germanic fertility goddess Eostre, and is often used among modern Wiccan groups. Ostara is ostensibly a modern take on the spring equinox, based on ancient springtime rites associated with growth, new life and fertility. The festival is marked by lighting bonfires, decorating eggs, and honouring Eostre, whose symbols include the hare and eggs. All these motifs symbolise springtime, the hatching of ideas, and striding out into the sunshine with a real spring in our step to empower us for the months ahead. Little is known about Eostre herself, but she is most likely a Maiden aspect of the Triple Goddess.

One legend states that she found a bird with a broken wing and, to save it, turned it into a hare, which still had the power to lay eggs. In Germanic myth, Eostre is associated with fertility rites and the moon. It has been debated whether the worship of Eostre is linked to the naming of the Christian festival of Easter, which falls on the first Sunday after the full moon that occurs on or after the spring equinox.

Many ancient sacred sites throughout the world are aligned with the equinoxes and/or solstices. In Britain, several Neolithic burial mounds align with the spring and autumn equinoxes. At the Avebury complex in England, the West Kennet Longbarrow chamber aligns with the rising sun at the spring equinox. This was thought to be a site where ancient peoples celebrated the spring and the sun's life-giving power as part of the never-ending cycle of life and death.

A SPRING EQUINOX SUN SALUTATION

To align with and show your appreciation for the equinox, at any time during the equinox day, perform this simple sun salutation to give thanks for the sun's life-giving force, and to feel a connection to universal energy.

1. Face in the direction of the sun, but don't look directly at it. Stand still, let your arms fall naturally by your sides and cultivate a sense of calm.
2. When you feel ready, raise your arms above your head and entwine your fingers, with palms facing the sky.

45

3. Hold this pose for thirty seconds while you imagine the moment of equal night and day across the world.

4. Thank the sun for its magical power, then loosen your grip and sweep your arms down and in front of your chest to make a prayer pose, with your hands pointing to the sun.

5. Next, open your arms as wide as you can, like a set of scales. Hold the pose for a few moments, and imagine that you are balancing and creating harmony throughout the world.

6. Now bring your hands together as if embracing the world to your chest. Swivel round 180 degrees so your back is to the sun, and again raise your arms with your hands entwined. Repeat steps 3–6 then raise your arms to the sky again.

7. Before you drop your arms back to your sides, thank the sun for showing you the light and dark sides of the Earth, and for the blessing of its ever-growing light on this vernal equinox day.

EQUINOX DAY RITUAL

Whether you decide to give thanks to the spring goddess, Eostre, or simply celebrate the vernal equinox, enjoy this equinox day ritual to acknowledge and appreciate the beauty and power of nature at this time of year.

You will need:

spring flowers and seasonal plants, such as daffodils, pots
   of spring bulbs, a jug of cow parsley or wild garlic leaves
7 hard-boiled eggs
4 yellow tealight candles
4 pieces of citrine

1. Begin by creating a sacred altar decorated with your spring plants and flowers. Add the Celtic symbol of growth and transformation to your altar: the egg. Decorate the shells of seven hard-boiled eggs (seven is the number of mystical power) with words, symbols or images that inspire you for the future.

2. Arrange the eggs on your altar to mark the points of a six-pointed star (hexagram), with the last egg in the centre to maximise the power of the hexagram. Whether you celebrate with friends or alone, stand before your dedicated space and give thanks to the Sun God for his life-giving power, and to the Earth Goddess for her fertility and her eggs.

3. Later in the day, treat yourself to a special celebratory spring bath, surrounded by spring flowers such as daffodils. Place a yellow tealight candle and a piece of citrine at each corner of the bath. Safely light the candles, then sink into your bath to relax and honour this time of balance, growth, rejuvenation and anticipation for the months to come.

4. Bury one of your seven eggs every day for a week in your garden, or compost/recycle them responsibly,

as a symbol of giving back what is taken from the earth, and to promote inspirational ideas for the future.

AN EGG BLESSING

The egg is a universal symbol of fertility and rebirth, and in Celtic tradition it is said to be made up of the four elements – the outer shell corresponds to earth, the membrane signifies air, the yolk corresponds to fire, and the white connects with water.

You will need:
1 hard-boiled egg
1 bottle of food colouring of your choice
seasonal flowers

1. Decorate your egg by dyeing it with the food colouring, then place it on your altar surrounded by seasonal flowers.
2. Focus on the egg for a few moments to find stillness, and then begin to visualise yourself deep within the yolk, filled with the element of fire.
3. You are now coming to life. You break out of the flaming interior, through the white of water, and pass the membrane of air, which gives you breath.
4. You see the outer shell, and can sense the element of earth as you say: 'I will break through the shell and awaken to the light of spring.'
5. Touch the egg, and be aware of your touch as you

are infused with the solar energy of the equinox and spring.

6. Take the egg in both hands and hold it close to your belly. Thank the egg, the Earth Goddess and Sun God for their blessing as you replace the egg on your altar. Leave it there for as long as you feel is right. It will remind you of your own ability to break through restrictions and take a new direction in life.

BASK IN THE POWER OF THE SUN

1. To bask in the sun's enriching rays, stand outside on a bright day and let the warm, radiant energy of the sun permeate your body and soul.

2. As you stand still, contemplate the sun's vitality, luminosity and power. Let its rays fill you with light and empower you with the energy needed to pursue your desires and dreams.

3. When you feel revitalised, this meaningful ritual is complete. Extend your heartfelt thanks to the sun for all that it brings to our lives and gives to this planet.

MYTH

Wicca honours all deities from a wide range of pagan beliefs, especially nature gods and goddesses. March aligns with

Pan, the Greek Arcadian god of the wild, who blows off the dust from his magic pipes, holds the reed to his lips, and fills the woods with his music. This ancient deity is associated with the Horned God and Cernunnos, and, like all nature gods, he was infamous for lustily chasing after nymphs. One nymph, Pitys, fled his advances and was transformed into a tree, a mountain pine that became sacred to Pan. Another nymph, Syrinx, escaped him and was turned into a clump of reeds, from which Pan crafted his pipes in memory of the loss of his greatest love.

In Kenneth Grahame's novel *The Wind in the Willows*, Pan is the unnamed 'Piper at the Gates of Dawn'. In this brief story within a story, Pan is portrayed as a mysterious, elusive deity who helps animals in need. Two of the novel's protagonists, Rat and Mole, encounter Pan on a mysterious island after he has saved a friend of theirs, a young otter. But as if in a dream, the god's numinous presence fades, and they begin to forget his magnificence. As they row on down the river, Rat and Mole hear the faint music of pan pipes and a voice whispering to them from the reed beds: 'You shall look on my power in the helping hour – But then you shall forget.' And, then, of course, they do forget!

FORGET AND REMEMBER RITUAL

To celebrate Pan as he guide us through the gates of spring's dawn and puts to rest the dark hours of winter, try the following ritual.

1. Take a walk in nature to establish a better connection with the natural world. As you do so, form a small collection of twigs, pebbles, leaves and fallen blossoms that appeal to you.

2. Take a few moments to simply stop and listen. Close your eyes and open your heart to Pan's powerful energy.

3. Make an offering with what you've foraged on your walk by placing the collection beneath a tree with which you feel an affinity.

4. As you do so, thank Pan for bringing you safely to the gates of another spring dawn. Forget the dark, but remember the light that guided you to the present.

WICCAN MYTH CYCLE

Around the equinox days of March, the Earth Goddess is now preparing her boudoir, creating potions, flowers, aphrodisiacs and perfumes to bewitch the Sun God in the coming months. She knows, instinctively, that he is not far from her door. So for now, she runs through the woods, enjoying the freedom to dance with tree nymphs, Pan and the satyrs, and to lie among the spring flowers. The Sun God, who is now about halfway through his journey to the highest point of the sky in the northern hemisphere, is at last feeling in balance with the Earth Goddess. Their masculine and feminine energies, poised and harmonious, are awaiting the perfect moment to unite.

FULL MOON: CHASTE MOON

In the early Roman calendar based on the lunar cycle, March was considered the first month of the year, and so became known as the first or 'chaste' full moon. A temple known as the *aedes lunae* was built on the Aventine Hill in Rome, alongside temples dedicated to Ceres, Minerva and Diana, and officially opened in honour of the moon goddess, Luna, on 31 March. The month itself became sacred to Luna, who was depicted with a cloak of a thousand stars and a crescent moon tiara on her head.

LUNA'S RITUAL

Draw on the energy of the Chaste Moon in March to enhance Luna's qualities of love, instinct, intuition and nurture, and to unmask your own hidden qualities.

You will need:
a white tealight
a silver object, or a piece of moonstone or selenite

1. On the day of the full moon, find a clear space to safely light your white tealight.
2. Take your silver object, moonstone or selenite and place it in front of the tealight to invoke Luna's power.
3. To ask for Luna's blessing, say: 'Luna, thank you for your silver rays, connecting me to the shimmering moonlight that lies within me, stirring

self-love and creativity for the months to come. Blessed be.'

4. Blow out the candle when you feel ready, and keep your chosen sacred object underneath your pillow overnight to invite Luna's magical power into your life.

CONNECT TO NATURE

March is often associated with breezy days and windswept gardens. If there is one animal that seems to best symbolise the energy of March, it's the hare. Sitting low on its 'form' (a shallow nest in a field), it instinctively choses the best pathway to escape its predators, usually running uphill or upwind to avoid capture. In Wiccan witchcraft, this aligns with a simple ritual to see which of the hare's pathways to welcome into your life. At the same time, this will enable you to feel at one with nature.

WIND RITUAL

On a windy day in March, align yourself with the spirit of the season by using the direction of the wind to determine your path like the hare.

You will need:
a handful of seeds, petals or leaves
a few stones

1. Standing outside on a blustery day, face the prevailing wind and imagine you are as wild and free as the hare. As the wind picks up, feel it rustling your silky coat, creating soft ripples across your back. You, the hare, can move, leap and run, knowing instinctively the way to freedom.

2. Stand for a while, then make a note of which direction the wind is blowing from.

3. If the wind blows from the west, turn your back to the wind and scatter some seeds, fallen petals or leaves into the wind and say, 'Welcome, west wind. Help me to plant new ideas for the months ahead.'

4. If the wind blows from the north, toss a few stones into the wind, and say, 'Welcome, north wind. Help me to promote realistic ideas.'

5. If the wind blows from the east, turn to the wind and shout out into it, 'Welcome, east wind. Help me to encourage the power of my voice so that I can communicate successfully.'

6. If the wind blows from the south, turn to face the wind, spread your arms out wide as if to embrace the wind and say, 'Welcome, south wind. Help me to promote passion and love in my life.'

By harnessing the power of the wind's direction, you will know which of the hare's pathways you need to follow this spring.

STARLORE

As we move on through March, the brightest constellation you will see in the northern hemisphere is Ursa Major, or the Great Bear. Meanwhile, the Plough, an asterism of seven bright and visible stars that make up the bear's back and tail, will become a familiar signature in the night sky until the summer months. Both should be visible if you look northwards in the night sky before midnight. But how did the Great Bear become such a familiar, shining friend?

In Greek mythology, the promiscuous Zeus lusted after the nymph Callisto. Hera, Zeus's jealous consort, discovered that Callisto had a son, Arcas, and devised a plan to exact revenge on the nymph. Hera transformed Callisto into a bear, with the intention that Arcas, who was on a hunting trip, would unwittingly kill his own mother. But before Arcas could shoot the bear with his arrow, Zeus saved Callisto by placing her in the sky as the constellation Ursa Major. Arcas went on to become the King of Arcadia.

As the Maiden phase of the Earth Goddess is fading, and the goddess is transforming to her mothering aspect, perhaps when you glimpse Ursa Major, you will see not only a mother bear, but also the mother in yourself? Reflect perhaps on what the motherhood archetype means to you (without any gender attachment). Can you be genuinely compassionate to yourself and others? Are you the big bear who cares for all forms of life and embraces nature, or are you fearful of embracing the mother archetype?

TAROT: THE EMPEROR

As the sun moves through the zodiac sign of Aries, the Emperor Tarot card signifies this solar journey of empowerment and strength. The Emperor is strong, confident and courageous, and knows he will get what he wants, especially if he sticks to the rules. This card tells us that with a sense of personal authority and a real awareness of leadership, we can make progress – but if we are too dogmatic, insensitive or assertive, we may find we are challenged. Reflect on this card at the equinox and ask yourself how you may balance these qualities in your own life.

APRIL

'You know how it is with an April day
When the sun is out and the wind is still,
You're one month on in the middle of May.
But if you so much as dare to speak,
A cloud comes over the sunlit arch,
And wind comes off a frozen peak,
And you're two months back in the middle of March.'

ROBERT FROST,
'Two Tramps in Mud Time'

APRIL AT A GLANCE

THEMES	purpose, creative desires, practice
FESTIVAL/FOCUS	a time of preparation
DEITY	Flora
CRYSTALS	red carnelian/emerald
ELEMENTS	fire/earth
FULL MOON	Seed/Growing Moon
TREE	aspen
BIRD	swallow
PLANT	anemone
ZODIAC	Aries/Taurus
TAROT	the Hierophant

SEASON AND CYCLE

For many Wiccans, April is a time of preparation in readiness for the great festival of Beltane on 1 May. But there is always work to be done on oneself, so perhaps take some time to consider your current creative goals and how you might prepare and plan for manifesting them. Although April doesn't 'feel' much different to March weatherwise, as the sun moves through the fire element of Aries, it heralds a chance to draw on any opportunities for inspired thinking. Then, from around 21 April, as the sun enters earth-ruled Taurus, you'll begin to see ways to ground yourself and put your ideas into practice.

The origins of the name 'April' are disputed, with some believing that it may have derived from the Latin *aphrilis*, as the springtime aspect of Aphrodite/Venus was worshipped at this time of year. The great poet Ovid wrote in Book IV of *Fasti* (*Book of the Roman Calendar*, 8 CE): 'I have come to the fourth month, full of honour for you; Venus, you know both the poet and the month are yours.' Others have suggested that the naming of the month originates from another Latin word, *aperire*, meaning 'to open', which alludes to the blossoming of flower buds. Meanwhile, two other springtime goddesses have festivals that take place in April: Flora, the Roman goddess of flowers, and the Phrygian Cybele, known as Magna Mater (the Great Mother) by the Romans.

The beautiful star of the woods, the anemone, is at its best at this time, as rivals begin to appear beneath the canopy of trees. Sweet violets dot the shade, and carpets of bluebells begin to illuminate the woodland. Trees and hedgerows are in leaf or blossom, and swallows delight us as they begin to return to their homes after a long flight from southern Africa. Robins, blackbirds, tits and finches join in the first ubiquitous dawn chorus. However, Mother Nature can still be capricious, and there is a distinct ambivalence to the April weather. Perhaps this is because we are standing on the threshold between the first arousal of the equinox, and the climax of Beltane with its sensual overtones of passion, love and fertility. In all, April is a time for preparation, anticipation and awareness of joy to come.

LIBIDO RISING

In medieval European courts, spring was believed to be an auspicious time for couples to conceive a male heir. It was a popular tradition to celebrate male virility, prowess and fertility as Beltane approached. Court sorcerers would be kept busy concocting phallic stimulants and potions for high-born women to ensure the birth of a male to continue the patriarchal line. It was, of course, believed that the gender of the child was entirely down to the mother.

CELEBRATING APRIL

There is no Wiccan festival in April, although some Wiccans celebrate the Eve of Beltane (30 April), which coincides with the Roman celebrations of the goddess Flora (see page 63). For the first three weeks of the month, which are ruled by the fire sign Aries, we may feel a sense of heightened motivation, while in the last ten days, we feel more grounded as the sun moves through the earth element sign of Taurus, signifying a time when pleasure can be found in trying out our creative ideas.

Begin by considering what you would like to accomplish or create, and once you have a goal in mind, you can dive in to one of the following rituals to inspire you if you are searching for fresh ideas and creative results.

A RITUAL FOR SIBYL INSPIRATION

The Megalesia was a lavish Roman celebration at the start of April for the ancient Phrygian and Greek mother goddess, Cybele, known as Magna Mater by the Romans. Along with Apollo and Ceres, Cybele was one of three deities accorded power in the *Sibylline Books* (c. sixth century BCE), a collection of Greek oracular verses that was regarded as a highly important text by the Romans and consulted during moments of crisis over the course of the Empire (not to be confused with the *Sibylline Oracles* of a later date). Cybele's divine words were spoken by the Cumaen sibyl, one of Apollo's oracular priestesses, who resided in a cave in Cumae, a Greek settlement on mainland Italy.

Why not petition Cybele for divine inspiration so that you can act as your own sibyl?

Divination is the act of drawing on divine energy for those who seek enlightenment and purpose. A simple form of the practice that I like to use involves selecting a book by chance that will then act as a tool to help discover inner truths.

1. Go to your local bookshop or library. Let yourself be drawn to a section: it doesn't have to be a genre or area that you would usually gravitate towards.

2. Close your eyes and run your hand along the spines. Carry on running your hand back and forth until you intuitively sense the moment is right to stop.

3. Open your eyes and take out the book.

4. Now close your eyes again and open the book at a page that feels right. With your eyes still closed, run your finger along the open page and stop again.

5. Now open your eyes and read the passage that your finger is pointing to, or the one closest to it if you happen to land on an illustration.

6. This is the passage for your creative inspiration. Make a note of the text and consider the ideas that it presents to you over the coming days, as this will offer you the insight needed for any new creative endeavour.

The *Sibylline Books* were also consulted after a drought occurred in the area surrounding Rome from 241–238 BCE. Following the books' advice, a temple dedicated to Flora, the goddess of flowers, was erected in Rome, and the Floralia, a festival celebrated at the end of April, was established. The festival included the *ludi florae* (Flower Games), which involved six days of feasting, licentious mayhem, nakedness and erotic dancing.

In addition to flowers, Flora (Chloris in Greek mythology and the wife of the west wind, Zephyrus) was also the goddess of spring, youth and fertility. Known mostly for Botticelli's allegorical portrayal of her in the painting *Primavera*, as well as a later depiction by the Pre-Raphaelite artist Evelyn de Morgan, Flora is the embodiment of spring. She is the blossom in the trees, the wildflowers underfoot and the buds bursting into life all around you.

CREATIVE ABUNDANCE RITUAL

To enhance the abundant flowering of your own springtime intentions, connect with Flora's bountiful energy.

You will need:
a small bunch of seasonal flowers or herbs
a replica of Botticelli's *Primavera*

1. Place your seasonal flowers or herbs and your replica of *Primavera* on your altar.

2. Take a few long, deep breaths, find stillness, and focus on the painting, imagining you are a part of this allegory of spring. To the right of the painting, Zephyrus kidnaps the nymph Chloris, who is transformed into the goddess of spring Flora, her robe studded with flowers. Venus looks on with Cupid, and they are joined by the three Graces and, to the far left, Mercury, who raises his staff to the stars.

3. This imagery symbolises transformation as we move through the spring season, and is analogous to our own personal myth unfolding.

4. For a few minutes, meditate on your own story and how you see your creative power manifesting, then scatter a few petals or flowers across the painting to symbolise your connection to the creativity of springtime.

5. Give thanks to Flora by saying: 'Thanks be to you, goddess of flowers, fertility, youthfulness, beauty and grace, for your abundance at this springtime. Blessed be.'

6. Keep the painting and flowers on your altar until Beltane (1 May) to encourage a fertile creative mind and usher in an abundant summer.

THE CUMAEN SIBYL

The Cumaen Sibyl was thought to write oracular symbols on oak leaves, which were arranged to form a message and left at the entrance of her cave. When a seeker entered the cave, the leaves would often blow away due to a draught or breeze, so the message would be disturbed and the querent would leave without an answer. If, however, the seeker could enter without disturbing the leaves, they would be gifted a divine message that would reveal their destiny. According to legend, the Sibyl had nine prophetic books which foretold the future of Rome. The last semi-mythical king of Rome, Tarquinius Superius, was desperate to buy the books, but the Sibyl's price was too high. Because he refused her offer, she threw three books into the fire, then made a counter offer. This, too, he declined, so she burned three more books. With only three books left, Tarquinius had no choice but to pay the full amount for the remaining three, which were kept on the Capitoline Hill in Rome, until they were destroyed in a fire in 83 CE.

RED CARNELIAN SPELL

Red carnelian is the stone assigned to Aries, and the Celts associated it with leadership, strength and success. The stone was worn by warriors to promote fearlessness in battle, while great kings and queens used it for empowerment. This simple spell will encourage confidence, clarity and courage.

You will need:
a piece of red carnelian

1. Simply keep the piece of red carnelian with you for the first three weeks of April.
2. Each day, hold the stone between your hands as you affirm, 'This stone empowers and bestows me with the knowledge of my own success.'
3. When the sun moves into Taurus (check the day in an ephemeris, see glossary) place the stone in a safe place in your home and keep it there until the following year, when you can repeat the ritual. You will now be filled with confidence and success for the coming months.

MYTH

The willow tree has long been a symbol of wisdom and flexibility, and according to the Celtic tree calendar, it is associated with April.

The willow's lunar month, which ran from mid-April to mid-May, was known to the Celts as Saile (pronounced 'Sahl-yeh'). In ancient Greek mythology, the willow was sacred to the goddesses Hera, Hecate, Circe and, in some accounts, Persephone, who was said to tend a grove of willows and black poplars in the underworld. It was thought that Orpheus (see page 71) was given the gift of his beautifully bewitching voice when he touched a willow tree in Persephone's grove. In Wicca, the willow tree is also associated with Brigid, the

Maiden element of the Triple Goddess, while in Celtic and Druidic lore, the universe hatched from two crimson serpent eggs (one the sun, the other the Earth) that were hidden among the boughs of a willow tree.

In European folklore, the wise willow is associated with healing, the moon, femininity, new life and growth. A renowned wood for weaving and wickerwork due to its incredible pliability, the willow was also used for protection against negative energy. A willow planted near the home was believed to protect against natural disasters, particularly 'water elemental spirits' who might invoke storms and floods.

WILLOW RITUAL FOR PROTECTION

You will need:
15 willow leaves

1. Arrange the willow leaves in a circle around you and stand in the middle.
2. Give thanks to the willow for its protective influence.
3. Gather up your willow leaves and leave them in a prominent position in your home to benefit from their protective power.

WICCAN MYTH CYCLE

As the Sun God travels on through the fire sign of Aries, he becomes more aware of his potent masculinity and his power to bring more light to the world. He is at his most virile while in Aries, the sign of the rampant ram. As he moves on into the sensual earthiness of Taurus, he is now also known as the Lord of the Wildwood and god of the forests, awaiting his encounter with the Earth Goddess in her Maiden form. The fecund Sun God prepares to sow his seeds, knowing the forthcoming union will bring fertility to all the earth. The Earth Goddess is anticipatory, bathing in sensual oils, weaving garlands of flowers for the love bower, and drawing on magic charms as she awaits the Beltane union.

FULL MOON: SEED/GROWING MOON

This month's full moon, known as the Growing Moon or Seed Moon in Celtic and other pagan traditions, embodies April's spirit of growth. It is associated with new beginnings and setting intentions, and is a time when our spirits are uplifted and nature flourishes around us.

GROWING INTO MYSELF VISUALISATION

1. On the day of the full moon, sit beside a flower in bud. Even if its growth is not visible to the naked eye, know that every second it is slowly evolving, as the bud or leaf unfurls at its own pace until the time is right for it to be fully open.
2. Close your eyes and imagine that, like the flower bud, you are growing too. Become aware of how,

with each passing day, you are discovering more about yourself and the person that you would like to become.

3. Next, open your eyes and inspire yourself with the energy of spring and nature's blessing by repeating:

> 'I am at one with the wind, trees, sky and moon.
>
> I am at one with nature and the divine that flows through the flowers.
>
> I grow with the universe, for all the universe is within me.'

4. To continue charting your journey of growth, you may want to keep a journal or write down the above phrase in your Book of Shadows.

CONNECT TO NATURE

SWALLOWS

In early Neolithic art, the Great Goddess was often identified as a bird goddess. Birds are associated with air in the elemental pentagram, and are thought to lead us directly to an understanding of our own ethereal spirit if we observe, welcome and appreciate their magical power. If you have the chance and opportunity to see the first swallows arriving home, stand and watch as they swoop across the sky. To feel more connected to this archetypal symbol of devotion, freedom, peace and good luck, imagine their incredible journey. Swallows fly over six thousand miles, starting in sub-Saharan Africa and finally reaching the UK. These awe-inspiring birds fly almost non-stop for around six weeks, covering roughly two hundred miles a day, in order to return to their homeland.

SWALLOW RITUAL

To align to the swallow's natural freedom and this magical bird's message of positive change for the future, try this lunar springtime practice.

You will need:
a piece of paper and a pen
5 white tealight candles

1. During the waxing moon phase in April, draw five swallows in the pattern of a pentagram on a piece of paper and place on your altar or table. On each swallow, place a white tealight candle.
2. Light the candles carefully, then say: 'When I draw on the love of the swallows, I am setting myself free from all negativity, and am at one with spirit, air, earth, fire and water.'
3. Focus on each candle flame for a few moments and, when you feel intuitively ready, blow them out and remove the candles.
4. Take your swallow pentagram and keep in a safe place. If you ever need to feel as free as a bird, take

your swallow motifs and hold the paper to your heart for a few moments as you imagine yourself soaring above the world.

STARLORE

The meteor showers known as the Lyrids occur every year in mid to late April. The shower gets its name from the constellation Lyra, the point in the sky from which the meteors appear to originate. The Lyrids aren't quite as spectacular as the Perseids of August, but their unpredictable trajectories and erratic timing are fascinating to observe.

The constellation Lyra represents the lyre of Orpheus, a musician and poet in Greek mythology. Apollo had given the young Orpheus a golden lyre, and Orpheus's musical skill was so profound that it was said he was able to charm even stones with his music. Orpheus was ultimately ripped apart by the Maenads, the female followers of Dionysus, because they felt spurned and enraged that after the loss of his wife, Eurydice (see below), he chose to take only male lovers. The Maenads also threw his lyre into the river in their anger, and so Zeus sent an eagle to retrieve it. To honour the musician and his instrument, Zeus placed them both in the sky as constellations. Lyra is also home to one of the brightest stars, Vega. In the northern hemisphere, this beautiful bluish star can be seen by looking north-eastward. Even on a full moon night, Vega is still visible.

On a clear evening, as you gaze up at Lyra in the night sky, try listening to classical pieces inspired by Orpheus, such as Offenbach's *Orpheus in the Underworld* or Gluck's *Orpheus and Eurydice*. If you spot the Lyrids, take a moment to think about Orpheus's desire to reunite with his lost wife. As the story goes, Orpheus travelled to the underworld in search of Eurydice, who had perished after being bitten by a snake. Petitioning Hades, god of the underworld, for his wife's return, Orpheus played music so sweet that Hades assented and allowed Orpheus to bring her home on one condition – he was not allowed to look back at her until they had reached the mortal world. On approaching the end of their journey, however, Orpheus could not resist the temptation of one fleeting glance, and thus Eurydice was lost for ever.

Perhaps Orpheus's folly is a reminder that we must keep moving forwards, as to look back will only make us live in regret.

TAROT: THE HIEROPHANT

The Hierophant aligns to this month's theme of preparation and readiness. The wisdom of the Hierophant (a priest or priestess who interprets sacred mysteries) asks you to take time to find your own inner truth. This card also represents showing respect for other beliefs and traditional practices, and asks you to be sure of your core values and commitment to your goals. April is a time to consider the Hierophant within; to trust in your own authenticity so you are prepared and ready to walk down your chosen pathway.

MAY

'Love, whose month is ever May,
Spied a blossom passing fair
Playing in the wanton air.'

WILLIAM SHAKESPEARE,
Act IV, Scene 3, *Love's Labour's Lost*

MAY AT A GLANCE

THEMES	fertility, love, play, the sacred feminine
FESTIVAL/FOCUS	Beltane (1 May)
DEITY	Maia
CRYSTALS	emerald/citrine
ELEMENTS	earth/air
FULL MOON	Hare/Bright Moon
TREE	hawthorn
BIRD	kestrel
PLANT	bluebell
ZODIAC	Taurus/Gemini
TAROT	the Lovers

SEASON AND CYCLE

Nature seems to burst into life with the arrival of May. We can almost hear and smell the Beltane bonfires being lit, feel the sensual energy as folk swirl around maypoles, and envision the forthcoming marriage of the Earth Goddess to the Sun God, who at this time of year is often identified with the Horned God or Lord of the Greenwood.

May is a time to honour all things fertile, virile, pleasurable and playful, and it is believed to be named after the goddess Maia (see page 84). The sun moving through Venus-ruled Taurus encourages greater opportunities for establishing romantic and intimate relationships, and this is followed by the light-hearted, joyous fun to be had as we move into frivolous Gemini on around 20 May. This is a month when the dawn chorus speaks louder than words – 'When every lusty heart beginneth to blossom, and to bring forth fruit' (Sir Thomas Malory, *Le Morte D'Arthur*).

A fertile time for the natural world, May is when love quickens and hearts flutter. We romance to the tune of the season, knowing that there is not actually that long left before the retreat of the sun. But for now, the hawthorn unfolds its buds, swifts cruise silently across the brightening skies, bluebells and wild garlic carpet the woodland floor, and wafer-thin beech leaves begin to unfurl. It's time to make love unfurl for you, too, and that means loving yourself and those who matter, and showing your love and respect for nature and the sacredness of you, your loved ones and the whole of the world.

THE CHARGE OF THE GODDESS

An essential Wiccan text known as the 'Charge of the Goddess' (of which there are various versions) is used in many rituals to remind initiates of the messages of love and gratitude given by and to the Earth Goddess. In Wiccan High Priestess Doreen Valiente's version of the text, we are reminded that the Goddess (in all her emanations) is to be invoked during Beltane celebrations: 'All acts of love and pleasure are her rituals.' This is the time of year to find your joy, whether physical, creative or spiritual.

CELEBRATING MAY

BELTANE

During Beltane, nature is fertile and abundant, and there is a palpable heightened sexual energy. This is a time for loving commitments, and encouraging intimacy through the gathering of May blossom (see page 80). The word 'Beltane' is believed to originate from the Celtic celebration of the god

Belenus or Bel, meaning 'the bright one', and *teine* meaning 'fire'. Bel was a powerful sun god, and during the summer, bonfires would be lit in his honour to petition him to protect cattle put out in the pastures. In Celtic Ireland, fires were often lit high up on a hill to represent the local community's collective worship of the Sun God. A torch was lit from the fire and taken to the heart of the village, and from this beacon, each home would light their own torch (as is also done at Samhain), and then use it to rekindle the hearth with the Sun God's blessing for the months to come.

For most contemporary Wiccans, Beltane is a celebration of the fertile marriage of the Earth Goddess and the Sun God (in whatever guise they are known to local groups). It is a time where everyone can enjoy giving love and receiving the love of others. Traditional ways to celebrate include the nineteenth-century Celtic folk ritual of procuring a 'May bough'– usually a bough of hawthorn flowers, often still in bud, that would be placed, along with rushlights, outside the house until the end of May to bring luck and fertility to all.

To the ancient agrarian Celts, there were only two seasons, summer and winter. Beltane marked the end of winter and the beginning of summer, and in their mythology, this was also a time to honour the aos-sí, supernatural 'little people' or fairies. In Celtic mythology, there is a triad of sacred magical trees: oak, ash and thorn (hawthorn). Hawthorn is the tree of fertility, oak of strength, power and longevity, and ash of growth, healing and rebirth. If you were to come across a sacred triad of an oak, an ash and a hawthorn tree, it was believed that, at Beltane, you would encounter spirits, fairies and other supernatural folk there.

HANDFASTING AND JUMPING THE BROOM

To celebrate the marriage of the Earth Goddess and Sun God, lovers would engage in the ritual of handfasting, in which their hands would be bound together, usually with a piece of cloth or cord, as a pledge of their love and fidelity. This commitment was intended to last for only a year and a day, so that the couple could choose whether to stay together or part after that time. Handfasting is still performed today, with ribbons used to bind hands together, but the promise of 'a year and a day' is usually now replaced with a vow suggesting a commitment for as long as the couples' hearts remain as one. At the end of the Beltane celebration, the hands are untied to show that the couple have agreed to remain together of their own free will.

Another popular folk ritual, known as 'jumping the broom', can also be used to demonstrate a couple's commitment to one another. The ritual is a simple one and involves laying a broom on the floor for the couple to jump over together. The jump symbolises a move from their old lives as individuals to their new life as a pair.

GOING A-MAYING

Traditionally, young people would go out into the local fields and woods to collect May blossom (hawthorn) on May Day eve, returning home at sunrise carrying flowering branches. The May tree was believed to be a source of sacred power, and it was considered inauspicious to bring its blossoms into the home on any day other than May Day. It is often alleged that going a-maying was also an opportunity for young couples to engage in clandestine physical intimacy, which is alluded to in the poem 'Corinna's Going a Maying' by the seventeenth-century English poet Thomas Herrick.

HAWTHORN OR BLACKTHORN?

If you decide to go a-maying, take care not to confuse May blossom with blackthorn. Although the two may look similar, you can easily recognise each plant by remembering that May blossom flowers will only appear after leaves have formed, while blackthorn blossom appears *before* the leaves form. Hawthorn is the tree of the Earth Goddess, while blackthorn is associated with the Dark Goddess (see page 189), and is believed to bring bad luck if brought into the home.

THE BOX OF DESIRES RITUAL

One of the great Celtic goddesses associated with Beltane is Danu, who coupled with Bel and was mother of the Tuatha Dé Danann, supernatural beings of Irish myth. The first of May celebrates the time when these gods were believed to have arrived in Ireland. Danu was originally a Hindu deity, and was believed to encourage one's true intentions to manifest. This is a traditional witchcraft ritual in which you can call on Danu and Bel to bless you with good intentions as you create a symbolic box of desires to manifest the things in life you truly long for. The Beltane energy fertilises thoughts and desires, preparing them to bloom in the coming months.

You will need:
a decorative box
at least one of the following objects:
piece of rose quartz or garnet (love or commitment)
copper coin (career)
citrine (abundance)
acorn or oak leaf (perseverance)
thimble (home harmony)
sprig of rosemary or a sage leaf (truth)
three-stranded braid of two green ribbons and one blue ribbon (vitality)
cinnamon stick (good luck)
gold ring (knowledge)
sketch of a treasure chest with the name of a lost item written on it (to find a lost item)
a metal key (protection)

1. Place your chosen object(s) in the box and give thanks to Bel and Danu for bringing you their Beltane good fortune by saying: 'Blessed Bel and Danu, thank you for bestowing on me good intentions, and for helping me to manifest my desires, so mote it be.'
2. Close the container and keep it on your altar to encourage your desires to be fulfilled during the

course of the rest of the year. You can change, add or remove items, as and when the desire manifests.

A MAYPOLE RIBBON RITUAL

You can do this traditional Wiccan ritual on any day in May to enhance all aspects of fertility (that includes fertility of the mind as well as the body, such as new ideas and creative inspiration).

A maypole is said to symbolise both the Earth Goddess and Sun God. Traditionally, the phallic pole (the Sun God) was decked with a ring of flowers (the fertile Goddess), while the coloured ribbons woven around and around the pole symbolise their union.

You can recreate the energy and magic of this ancient fertility dance with this braiding ribbon ritual, which uses the same colours traditionally used for weaving the maypole: green for growth, abundance and fertility; red for strength, vitality, passion and vibrancy; and white for cleansing, purifying and the power to disperse negativity.

You will need:
green, red and white ribbons (each about 60–90 cm/2–3 feet long)
rose petals, lavender flowers or the essential oil of your choice

1. Tie the ribbons together at one end and weave into a braid. When you're finished, tie off the other end.

2. Place your braid outside overnight to connect to the energy of the sun and moon.
3. The following day, untie the braid and loosen the ribbons.
4. Lay the three ribbons vertically on your altar, then sprinkle them with your rose petals, lavender flowers or essential oil and affirm: 'These ribbons imbue me with all forms of fertility throughout this turn of the Wheel of the Year.'
5. Leave in place until the end of May to invite more love and joy into your life.

MYTH

Two goddesses take central stage in May for their healing and wish-fulfilment powers: the Roman goddess Maia, after whom the month is named, and Sulis, the Celtic goddess of sacred springs and wells, who was syncretised into Roman mythology as Sulis Minerva after the Romans discovered her hot springs in Bath, England. We can draw on both these goddesses for their springtime magic to make good wishes for the coming season.

Sulis was originally a solar deity, and at her sacred springs at Bath, rituals were held to invoke her healing powers, while coins, jewels, amulets and 'curse' tablets (written petitions seeking revenge on wrongdoers) were cast into the hot springs for healing, hope and retribution.

Daughter to Atlas and Pleione, the Greek goddess Maia was the eldest of the seven nymphs known as the Pleiades (the well-known asterism in the constellation of Taurus). The word 'Maia' translates as 'great', 'mother' and 'nurse', and she was later adopted into the Roman pantheon and associated with growth, the earth and the month of May. She was identified with Roman earth goddesses, such as Terra and Bona Dea, and is also linked to the god Vulcan – the priests at the temple of Vulcan were thought to sacrifice a pregnant sow in honour of Maia on 1 May. In Greek mythology, she was a shy goddess who avoided Olympus, choosing instead to live alone in a cave near the peak of Mount Cyllene in Arcadia. After an ambiguous romantic encounter with Zeus, Maia secretly gave birth to Hermes, the god of wish fulfilment. By channelling Maia's magic as the mother of the month of May and Hermes, and the healing good wishes of Sulis, you can make your own wishes come true.

A RITUAL FOR MAIA AND SULIS

1. On a clear evening in May, find a peaceful spot outside. For a moment, stand with your eyes closed, make two full turns, and then open your eyes.

2. Look up at the sky, focus on the first star you see, and try to forge a sense of connection. As you do so, say: 'Thank you, Maia, for bringing the light of Hermes into my life and encouraging this wish to come true. Blessed be.' Now make your wish.

3. On the next clear night, go out and look up to the stars again, then choose another star and repeat your wish, this time giving thanks to Sulis, whose

healing and wish-fulfilment powers can encourage your own wish to come true.

WICCAN MYTH CYCLE

The Sun God and the Earth Goddess begin to court one another in the meadows and copses. The Sun God is virile, his ardour growing; he is potent and charged with pure sexual energy as he seeks out the Earth Goddess. It is in an enchanted green wood that their union takes place, while bonfires are lit to honour the god's ardour. The Earth Goddess beckons him to her, knowing that while he is the Lord of the Spring, his power is great, but soon that potency will fade away.

FULL MOON: HARE/BRIGHT MOON

In many world mythologies, the hare is considered a symbol of abundance, prosperity and good fortune. Associated with femininity, witchcraft, lunar cycles, fertility, longevity and rebirth, legends abound about the hare's contradictory nature. The magical hare symbolises both smart thinking and foolishness, fear and courage, and rampant sexuality and purity. In Germanic mythology, the hare was sacred to the spring goddess, Eostre, and in ancient Egypt, to the goddess Wenet.

The May full moon symbolises the magic, fertility and abundance associated with the hare. In English folklore, it was thought that if you saw a hare under the May full moon it was an auspicious sign, suggesting the potential for new beginnings or personal fortune.

HARE MOON RITUAL

Found in sacred sites from the Far East to medieval Christian churches, a sacred circular motif of three hares sharing only three ears creates an optical illusion. Like many symbols that depict a trinity (for example, the triskelion of Celtic mythology, which represents the past, present and future embraced in the present moment), the symbol of the three hares is believed to represent the lunar cycle of waxing, full and waning moon, echoed in the Wiccan Triple Goddess motif. The hare's magical power could thus be called upon at whatever moment of the cycle you are in. During a full moon, when aligned with citrine, it draws prosperity to you. So try out this medieval witchcraft ritual to connect with the sacred hare motif and encourage abundance.

You will need:
3 pieces of citrine
a flower or leaf of your choosing
a 30 cm (12 in) length of twine or ribbon

1. On the eve of the full moon, find a flat surface and form a triangle with your citrine that points north.
2. In the middle of the triangle, place the flower or leaf, and then form a circle around the triangle using your length of ribbon or twine to seal the petition.

3. Give thanks to the moon and the hare for helping you to fulfil a goal or desire by saying the following: 'Thank you, goddess of the moon, and the spirit of Hare, for with these symbols I make the circle complete, and with your light, send me this night a pathway to abundance. Blessed be.'

4. Leave the formation in place overnight to draw down the power of the Hare Moon to encourage prosperity and success.

CONNECT TO NATURE

As rowan trees are bedecked with foaming white flowers, cow parsley and buttercups spring up from seemingly nowhere to swamp verges and meadows alike. Mayflies rise and fall above warming ponds and rivers, and swifts and house martins continue to return from distant shores. May is not only the month for 'amaying', but also an opportunity to connect with nature in a unique way.

A RITUAL FOR ENCHANTMENT

You will need:
a handful of May blossom stems

1. Go to your front door and scatter the May blossom across your doorway so that it forms a boundary between interior and exterior.

2. Take a step forward so that one foot remains

indoors, while the other is positioned on the other side of the doorway.

3. Stay in this position while you say, 'I am on the threshold of nature's magic. Thanks to nature, I reconnect to the enchantment within me.'

4. You can now step fully over the May blossom, so that you are on the other side of the boundary. As you do so, say, 'I am part of the magic of nature, as the magic of nature is part of me.'

5. Gather the stems and place them outside your home to encourage nature's enchantment into your life every time you leave or enter.

STARLORE

As the second-largest constellation after Hydra, Virgo's increasing appearance in the night sky at this time of year once marked the early summer harvests in Europe. Virgo can be seen to the south, below Ursa Major, and is best spotted late in the evening, at about midnight. The ancient Greeks identified the 'Maiden' (i.e. Virgo) with Persephone, and also with Dike, goddess of justice and daughter of Zeus and Themis. Virgo is also sometimes linked to Astraeia, daughter of Astraeus (father of the stars) and Eos (goddess of the dawn). In fact, Virgo seems to represent an abundance of feminine archetypes.

In artistic depictions, Virgo is often shown with wings, holding an ear of wheat in her left hand that represents the constellation's brightest star, Spica (Latin for 'ear of grain').

When you gaze up at Virgo, try imagining any goddess of your choice looking down on you. As she raises that ear of wheat in the sky, let her remind you that it's time to plant your own metaphorical crops, whether of the mind, the body or soul.

TAROT: THE LOVERS

The Lovers card reflects the theme of Beltane: this is a time for commitment, whether that's to loving relationships or our dedication to caring for the natural world. The card asks us to consider the choices we have to make right now. One of the many interpretations of this complex card is that it is asking us to reflect a little more deeply before we make a decision. In a love triangle, we may be forced to choose one person over another, or we may have to choose between independence or forming an alliance. This card also asks us to reflect on what 'love' actually means to us.

JUNE

'I know a bank where the wild thyme blows,
Where oxlips and the nodding violet grows,
Quite over-canopied with luscious woodbine,
With sweet musk-roses and with eglantine.'

WILLIAM SHAKESPEARE,
Act II, Scene 1, *A Midsummer Night's Dream*

JUNE AT A GLANCE

THEMES	fulfilment, self-empowerment, awareness, vitality
FESTIVAL/FOCUS	summer solstice
DEITY	Áine
CRYSTALS	citrine/moonstone
ELEMENTS	air/water
FULL MOON	Mead Moon
TREE	elder
BIRD	red kite
PLANT	musk rose
ZODIAC	Gemini/Cancer
TAROT	the Chariot

SEASON AND CYCLE

June is named after the Roman goddess, Juno, who was the goddess of marriage and the protector of women and children, and was known as the Queen of Heaven. Wherever Juno went, her attendant, Iris (the personification of the rainbow), would follow, with her radiant robes trailing across the sky. In traditional folklore, June is often associated with rainbows, as the weather is often a mix of dazzling light from the high sun, followed by brief, heavy showers. Summer foliage and hedgerows thicken, green woodlands are dappled with pools of light, and the mystical nature of planet Earth is illuminated. On around 21 June each year, the sun reaches its zenith (the highest point in the sky) in the northern hemisphere, and this marks the longest day of the year, also known as the summer solstice. The term 'solstice' is derived from the Latin *solstitium*, which translates as the 'sun stands still'.

CELEBRATING JUNE

FESTIVAL: SUMMER SOLSTICE

In Wiccan and other pagan traditions, the summer solstice is a time to celebrate the sun's life-giving force, and also an opportunity for us to awaken to positivity and fulfilment, encouraging a healthy sense of ego. The day signifies both endings and new beginnings, and reminds us to be at one with the moment and to 'stand still' with the sun. For thousands of years, the summer solstice has been honoured and celebrated at sacred places throughout the world. Many ancient sites and structures align to the sun's rays during the solstices and equinoxes and, as most ancient peoples worshipped some form of solar deity, it is likely that it was at these sacred sites and at these awe-inspiring moments in the year that they gave homage to the Sun God.

At Stonehenge in Wiltshire, England, as the sun rises, its rays align perfectly with what is known as the Heel Stone (a standing stone that lies outside the circle), and then shine directly into the centre of the circle. Similar alignments occur at Newgrange in Ireland, the Egyptian pyramids, the Chichen Itza pyramid in Mexico, and the Great Serpent Mound in Ohio, USA. Standing stones, menhirs and stone circles are believed to have been constructed by ancient peoples to symbolise the cycle of life and death, and to honour the sun as life-giver.

In traditional Wicca, the summer solstice is a 'standing still' moment, when we can accept and appreciate our tiny place in the universe, and also express our love for one another, enhancing all aspects of our relationship with the natural world, of which we are a part. This time is the culmination of the Sun God's fecundity and the Earth Goddess's reciprocation, and as such the summer solstice is an important marker in the Wheel of the Year, highlighting not only the power of the sun, but also our dependence on its life-giving energy. Now is a time to keep our own 'fires' burning, to tend to our own solar light within, and to acknowledge our current loves, goals and aspirations, as well as focusing on what we wish to achieve as the Wheel of the Year continues to turn.

Being out in nature will allow you to engage with the magic of the summer solstice, but you can also heighten your connection to the sun's power through the solstice rituals shared in this chapter.

LITHA

Most Wiccans refer to this awe-inspiring time as the summer solstice. The term 'Litha' was first coined in the 1970s by prominent Wiccan practitioner and author Aidan Kelly, who also named the spring equinox Ostara and the autumn equinox Mabon. These names are still controversial among Wiccan groups. According to Kelly, Litha was derived from medieval scholar and historian Venerable Bede's Anglo-Saxon names for the two months of the summer: 'early Litha', which corresponded to June, and 'later Litha', which corresponded to July. Personally, I like to use the more traditional name, 'summer solstice', but it is up to you which you choose.

THE OAK KING AND THE HOLLY KING

Throughout the UK on solstice day, a folk story is played out by two actors at pagan gatherings at various sacred sites. This is the so-called battle between the Oak King and the Holly King, the 'light' and 'dark' lords (both aspects of the Sun God), who are rivals for the love of the Earth Goddess at this time of year. The Oak King is the personification of summer, and the Holly King of winter, and every year their ongoing fight is celebrated on this festive day. The Oak King has already 'won the hand' of the Earth Goddess at Beltane, but the summer solstice marks the moment of the Oak King's slow decline until the autumn equinox and the rising power of the Holly King. At the autumn equinox the Holly King becomes the Earth Goddess's consort until the Oak King begins his rise to power again the following spring equinox.

SOLAR MOTIVATION RITUAL

Take inspiration from the sun and stand still for a moment. Allow yourself to enjoy the day, and become fired up with enthusiasm.

1. Unless you are doing this at the time specified for the moment of solstice in an ephemeris or astronomical almanac, you can do this on any day or at any moment you intuitively feel is right for you. So whether you're gardening, washing, cooking, eating, thinking or working, just stop.

2. Put down your 'tools' and stand for a minute to find calm and stillness. Now turn to the south (unless you are already facing south) and close your eyes.

3. Raise your hands into prayer pose (just in front of your chest). For two minutes, stay like this, totally still. Empty your mind; be aware only of your standing stillness.

4. You have now engaged in a solstice moment. You have stood still with the sun and, like the sun, you can now look forward to the next moment of standing still around the winter solstice. For now, you'll be motivated and inspired to enjoy the summer ahead.

CITRINE AND MOONSTONE SPELL FOR PSYCHIC EMPOWERMENT

The summer solstice brings us a sense of joyous completion, yet also alludes to the darker days of winter ahead. The crystals citrine and moonstone correspond to empowerment and intuition respectively, and were worn or carried by medieval occultists and witches to maximise their psychic power. They also represent the summer and the sun (citrine) and the winter and the moon (moonstone). To intensify your own sense of psychic and spiritual connection to the divine essence of summer – and later, winter – try this crystal spell at any time around the solstice day.

You will need:
a paper and pen, or a length of white ribbon
a piece of citrine
a piece of moonstone

1. In the centre of your sacred table or altar, create a circle with the ribbon, or draw one on a piece of paper. This circle represents the sun.
2. Place the moonstone to the north of the circle, and the citrine to the south. Place the forefinger of your dominant hand in the centre of the circle, and affirm:

    'I am north, south, east and west.
    My solar light shines here the best.
    Thus does the yearly wheel turn round,
    I move and flow, I am unbound.'

3. Pick up the two crystals, taking one in each hand, and hold them for a few minutes to connect you to the power of the ever-changing synergy of the solar and lunar cycles. Feel the way this forms a circuit of energy around and through you.
4. When you are ready, place the crystals in the centre of the circle. Leave for twenty-four hours

to activate your own mystical awareness and to enhance your synergy with the Sun God and the Earth Goddess (in her aspect as a lunar deity) throughout the year.

DISCOVER YOUR OWN SOLSTICE 'SUNSET POINT'

At this time, many Wiccans gather at various sacred sites throughout the world to give thanks to and honour the sun, the Sun God and Earth Goddess. Not all of us can visit a sacred site, but perhaps you can try to see a sunset or sunrise on the solstice day. Watching the sunrise on the summer solstice day is, of course, a mystical experience, but unless you are keen to get up really early in the morning, opt for the sunset, as you're more likely to be up late in the evening anyway!

Here's how to enjoy your own magical moment of sunset from a vantage point of your choice.

1. The day before the solstice, choose your own 'sunset point': this might be a comfortable position in your home, or another place where you can watch the sun set over a tree, a horizon, a building, or just behind the clouds. Make a note of what time the sun appears to set there (within ten minutes or so).

2. On the day, prepare your observation point. You might decide to take a favourite beverage or a cake, or perhaps you could bring a crystal, like a sunstone or a piece of clear quartz to draw down the last of this momentous day's solar power.

3. About five minutes or so before you have calculated when the sun will sink below your chosen point, just sit in stillness and wait.

4. When the sun begins to disappear below this horizon line, raise your glass or hold out your offering, and salute the sun. Watch it sink lower and lower; it seems to happen so quickly once you have a horizon or some line that it is crossing. If you have no view of the sun, or it's a cloudy day, then just imagine it sinking below the horizon point.

5. In a way, you are saying farewell to the Sun God, honouring his fading summer power, until you repeat this at winter solstice sunrise and salute the Sun God's rebirth.

DECORATE YOUR HOME FOR MIDSUMMER

Decorate your summer altar with roses, elderflowers and any other flowers that are in season. You might decide to include images of bees, butterflies and any other symbols of midsummer that you like. Make offerings to the midsummer goddess Áine (see page 103) with images of her attributes, such as wild horses, a gold-coloured comb, flowers such as meadowsweet or elderflower, and the first ears of corn.

CREATE A FLORAL CROWN

One folk tradition celebrating the fertility of the Sun God and Earth Goddess is to weave a floral crown. The flowers represent the Earth Goddess, while the stems and wreath itself represent the Sun God. The crown imbues the wearer with the blessing of the deities and a sense of being at one with nature.

The easiest method is to use a florist's wreath, but if you don't want to use wire, you can weave three thin stems of willow or other flexible branches into a braid, then shape into a circle and secure with twine or raffia. Alternatively, you can use a straw hat. Weave into this base any seasonal flowers or other plant life of your choice. And when you have finished your craft, place it on your own head – or someone else's, to share your good will – and give thanks to the Sun God and Earth Goddess for their blessing.

VERVAIN MAGIC

Known as the 'enchanter's plant' and 'herb of grace' in folklore, vervain has been used by witches and pagans for warding off evil influences, to invoke the power of prophecy, to bless the home, and also to draw down the power of the sun and stars. At this time of year, vervain is at its prime. You can use it to dress and sanctify your altar for the solstice by sprinkling its leaves, flowers or a few sprigs around a green candle. If you pick wild vervain for this purpose, give thanks to the plant as you do so.

To encourage future success, carry a few sprigs in a pouch on the day of the solstice to draw on the solar energy. Alternatively, gather a small bunch of the herb at midday and offer it up to the sun, then place it under your pillow to imbue you with insight and protection.

AN ENCOUNTER WITH BENEFICIAL SPIRITS

Most Wiccans believe that the summer solstice is a time when the veil of illusion which separates the spirit and mundane worlds fades away, and, if we so desire, we can glimpse or encounter spirits, fairies, nymphs and other numinous folk. Shakespeare's *A Midsummer Night's Dream* beautifully encapsulates this otherworldly realm and how it interacts with our own, echoing the traditional belief that it is in woodland glades and secret places where you are most likely to encounter these spirits. Here's how to connect to those helpful, kindly spirits wherever you are on solstice eve.

You will need:
a white tealight candle
a piece of clear quartz
a mirror

1. Call on the four directions and cast a circle of protection around you (see page 114) to ensure you connect only to positive spirits.
2. Light the candle, then place it and the crystal before the mirror. Sit before the mirror and call on the Earth Goddess by saying:

> *'By lighting this candle, I am blessed by the energy of the Earth Goddess. With this flame, I honour the divine that flows through me, the earth upon which I stand, and the turning of the Wheel. Blessed be. With this flame I can*

> *see through the veil of illusion, and see that*
> *the spirit world is here with me now.'*

3. Gaze at the light of the flame reflected in the mirror. You may see shapes, figures or shadows emerge then disappear, and you may notice other twinkling lights dancing in the crystal as you now look through the mirror and see into the other world.
4. When you are ready, reach out to the mirror and say, 'Thank you, good spirits, for the light you shine out to me, to keep me safe from harm. Blessed be.'
5. End the ritual by blowing out the candle, and hold the crystal in your hands for a minute to give you a sense of being grounded and back in the mundane world.

MYTH

The Irish/Celtic deity Áine is the goddess of midsummer, prosperity and fertility. According to Celtic legend, Áine was the daughter of Eogabail, and one of the Tuatha Dé Danann, a supernatural race of immortal fairy folk. Áine's palace is said to be hidden upon the sacred hill Cnoc Áine in Munster, an ancient Neolithic site also dedicated to an unspecified sun deity. Until the late nineteenth century, it was common to light straw torches and dance to the summit of Cnoc Áine to celebrate the summer solstice, before descending to the lower pastures with flaming brands, calling for Áine's blessings for healthy animals and crops.

Not far from the Cnoc Áine, you can find the enchanted

Lough Gur. This sacred lake is replenished by a series of underground springs, and it is thought that during the summer solstice and Samhain, Áine can be seen combing her golden hair as she sits by the edge of the lake. In some folklore, Áine is still referred to as the *leannán sídhe* ('fairy lover'), who takes mortal lovers and bestows them with the power of magic in exchange for eternal devotion. She is thought to rule over the light half of the year, while her sister, Grian, rules over the dark. Grian and Áine may both be aspects of an earlier ancient feminine sun deity.

A RITUAL BLESSING FOR ÁINE

You will need:
a handful of rose petals or elderflowers
a red tealight candle
a few drops of rose essential oil

1. Give blessing to the goddess of midsummer, Áine, by sprinkling a circle of rose petals or elderflowers around a red tealight. Drizzle a few drops of the essential oil on to the petals to imbue the sacred space with the scent of summer.
2. Light the candle carefully, and then say, 'Thank you, Áine, for the light of midsummer, which makes this a time of joy and peace. With gratitude for the plants that bloom, for the wildlife that flourishes, for all that is fertile. Blessed be.'
3. Take up a few petals in your hand, and offer them out as if to the goddess before you. Focus on the

petals for a few moments, then replace them on your altar, knowing that Áine is there with you to see you through the summer days.

WICCAN MYTH CYCLE

As the Sun God is at his most powerful, his union with the Earth Goddess is now fulfilled, and from this solstice moment he must return to the dark place from which he was born. At the zenith of his power, the Sun God stands on the edge of some invisible precipice. As the day turns from standing still to falling over, the Sun God begins his descent to the southern hemisphere, and the Earth Goddess, pregnant with his power, nurtures and grows his seed in the north. This is a time for both their union and their separation to be celebrated.

FULL MOON: MEAD MOON

Made from fermented honey, water, spices and yeast, mead has long been both a sacred and popular drink throughout traditional cultures worldwide. In the northern hemisphere, the first honey was usually harvested at about this time, giving rise to the name of this full moon (although some sources say the word 'mead' is identified with 'meadow'). Whatever the case, in the Minoan culture of Crete, the summer solstice marked the end of the honey harvest. Bees were sacred to the Minoans, and the humming of bees was thought to be the song of the Great Goddess, as her nymphs, the *melissae*, tended her hives. The Minoans celebrated the summer solstice by drinking mead, which was believed to increase fertility and augur success for the coming year. (Please note the Mead Moon is the full moon *closest* to the summer solstice, so technically, it can occur in the first week of July.)

A RITUAL TO EMBRACE THE MEAD MOON

Here's a ritual to help you enjoy the Mead Moon and embrace the bees' blessing of prosperity. Drink the power of the 'honey moon' into your life as you connect with the lunar energy.

1. On the evening of the full moon, gaze up in the direction of the moon (it doesn't matter if you can't actually see it).
2. Raise your hands above your head, then hold them out wide as if to embrace the moon. Now, gradually wrap your arms around yourself, as if holding on to the moon and drawing it towards you.
3. As you do so, say, 'Blessings to the moon of mead, come drink with me. To encourage success to come my way, fill me with power to bring prosperity. Blessed be.'
4. Hold on to the moon in this way for a few minutes, as you fill yourself with its success-bringing energy. Then slowly unwrap your arms from around you, let them fall to your sides, and bow your head in thanks to the moon. You have now encouraged the moon's blessings for the future.

CONNECT TO NATURE

June is all about rainbows, blue skies and unpredictable weather. The birds are preoccupied with rearing their young, the wild rose clambers fast through hedgerows, and elderflowers appear in frothy sprays. The first three weeks of June are busy with growing and seeding, but there's a lull in activity after the splendour of solstice. Mother Nature flounces her skirts, ready to settle in for a period of bold blossom, as fallow deer gingerly appear in magical dawns, and red valerian runs riot.

WILD ROSE REFLECTION RITUAL

1. Look out for wild roses in hedgerows – varieties such as musk, dog, eglantine and the invasive *rosa rugosa* all have beautiful petals, and some have the most exquisite scent.
2. As you gaze in wonder at the hedgerow filled with flowers, imagine you are looking at the beauty of yourself.
3. Say to the rose: 'The rose is me and I am the rose; we are both wild in spirit and sacred in soul.'
4. Find joy with your wild spirit and sacred soul – after all, it is your innate connection with nature that is being reawakened every time you see the beauty of yourself reflected in a rose, a flower, a tree, the sky and the stars.

With light swamping the northern hemisphere (the further north you go, there is no night as such at this time) it's hardly surprising that constellations don't stand out in the sky as they do in winter. But those you might spot include the Little Dipper, the asterism found in Ursa Minor. Formed by seven bright stars, its showcase star is Polaris, or the North Star, which marks true north and has played an important navigational role throughout history. Another constellation that you may spot at around midnight is Cassiopeia. It is smaller, and made up of five main stars in the shape of a sideways 'W'. It is named after the vain mythological queen married to King Cephus, and can be found to the south-east of the Plough, and visible when you face to the north.

Cassiopeia, the mother of Andromeda (see page 179), boasted that her daughter was more beautiful than the Nereids. This angered Poseidon, which led to Andromeda being chained to a rock, although she was thankfully saved from a sea monster by the hero Perseus. Cassiopeia was eventually transformed into a constellation by Poseidon. According to Roman author Hyginus (64 BCE–17 CE), although she is seated in a chair, as the 'sky turns', the chair appears to lie on its back, and Cassiopeia appears almost upside down: a punishment, perhaps, for her disrespect of the gods.

As you gaze at this rather simple little constellation, it may remind you that by respecting the deities, the stars and all of nature, we can stand tall, animated and beautiful, rather than being stuck in a chair like Cassiopeia.

TAROT: THE CHARIOT

The Chariot is often depicted as being driven by a warrior or a solar deity, and this card aligns with the moment of the summer solstice when the Sun God's power is at its height. The Chariot represents emotions, controlling others, being in the driving seat and standing up for your beliefs. It reminds us to rein in our desires, and be more aware of the consequences of our actions. It also tells us that sometimes, the direction we take instinctively may lead us to greater achievements.

JULY

'I am she that is the natural mother of all things.'

APULEIUS,
The Golden Ass

JULY AT A GLANCE

THEMES	creativity, abundance, enjoyment
FESTIVAL/FOCUS	a month to celebrate summer magic
DEITY	Ceridwen
CRYSTALS	selenite/sunstone
ELEMENTS	water/fire
FULL MOON	Hay Moon
TREE	lime
BIRD	house martin
PLANT	marigold
ZODIAC	Cancer/Leo
TAROT	Strength

SEASON AND CYCLE

In the early Roman lunar calendar of Romulus (the legendary founder and first king of Rome), July was the fifth of only ten months, and was known as Quintilius (meaning 'five'). It was later renamed after Julius Caesar. In Anglo-Saxon tradition, it was referred to as 'Heymonath' or 'Maed-monath', because it was the perfect time for haymaking and the meadows would be in full bloom.

For most Wiccans, July is an opportunity to prepare for Lammas or Lughnasadh, which falls on 1 August. Lughnasadh is a celebration where thanks is given to nature and the gods for the summer bounty, and it was traditionally an important marker for the beginning of the Celtic harvest season. We can apply this attitude to ourselves, and make a conscious effort to prioritise our pleasure and joy, the symbols of summer, before the coming harvest. Whether we laze in the sun or picnic in the woods, we can use this month to understand and nurture our creative potential.

The start of July is usually mellow and languid. Bumblebees can be found busying themselves in our gardens, while moths, butterflies and dragonflies take to the air. The birds are fairly quiet, except for the excited screeches of young swifts diving across rooftops.

As there are no Wiccan or important pagan festivals this

month, why not simply enjoy yourself and celebrate nature's summer magic? Wicca is respectful of individuals, so take this time to discover your own pathway for connection to the divine; creating your own spells or rituals is a powerful way to do this. To ensure you are blessed and protected before trying out a new ritual or spell of your own design, cast a sacred circle and call on the four directions before you begin – see below.

CELEBRATING JULY

CREATE A SACRED CIRCLE

Perform this ritual to cast a sacred circle when you are about to perform a spell or ritual, or when you are out in nature to help you feel more protected yet connected to all around you too.

1. In Wiccan tradition, the four directions – the four cardinal points of the compass, east, south, west and north – correspond to the four elements: east to air, south to fire, west to water and north to earth.

2. While standing turn to face each of the four directions, moving in a sunwise direction (in the northern hemisphere, start by facing east, and then turn to the south, and so on) and calling on the spirit of the direction and element at each point. You can use your own words, or repeat these traditional lines:

'I call on the spirit of the east and air, the sky and the stars to bless me.

I call on the spirit of the south and fire, the landscape and light to enlighten me.

I call on the spirit of the west and water, the seas, the moon and the waters of Earth to embrace me.

I call on the spirit of the north and earth, the stones and rocks, to support me.'

3. Once you have turned to each direction and called on these quarters, reach out your hand and, with your finger pointing out like a compass, draw an invisible circle around you three times in the same sunwise direction (east, south, west, north, then east again).
4. Give thanks to the Sun God and Earth Goddess for their protective blessing.
5. You can now try out any creative ritual or spell you have in mind, knowing you are protected.

ELEMENTAL ENERGY RITUAL

As the sun moves through Cancer and then Leo, the elements of water and fire are highlighted. In traditional Wicca, working with the elements amplifies our connection to the divine flowing through all things. Water energy encourages intuition, compassion and a genuine feeling of togetherness, whether with a close friend, a lover, family, community or clan. Fire energy re-energises our willpower and our desire, and encourages us to pursue our objectives.

Try out this simple ritual as the sun moves from water to fire on around 22 July (you may need to check the exact day, as it varies every year). Feel the flow of watery warmth as it moves outwards, expressing love and care for others, then feel it flow back, empowering you with self-worth.

You will need:
a selection of summer flowers
a bowl of water (or, if possible, sit beside a lake, the sea, or another body of water)

1. First, to show you are dedicated to the changing energy of the summer sun as it moves from water to fire, scatter some flowers or petals around you to form a circle of summer empowerment. Then say, 'Thank you, Sun God and Earth Goddess, for aligning me to the spirit of summer and the elements of water and fire.'

2. Next, sit or kneel before the water. Touch it with your finger and say, 'With water, I am blessed with the love for others and from others.'

3. Now, with your damp finger, point to the sun and say, 'With fire, I am blessed with the love of self, and now I can use this love to give more to myself, and to others.'

4. After this ritual, simply stay for a while where you are to be at one with your environment. You will begin to feel the mutual exchange of love between you and the world.

SUNSTONE RITUAL FOR ABUNDANCE

As the sun moves into fiery Leo on around 22 July, the end of the month is about abundance. Flowers and fruits burst forth from the Earth Goddess's cornucopia, and there is a bustle of excitement in the hedgerows as young fledglings learn to fly and feed.

Here's how to attract an abundance of love, joy, pleasure and anything else you desire for the rest of the summer. It's also a reminder for you in the dark of winter that there is always a summer to come around again, as the Wheel of the Year keeps on turning.

You will need:
a sunstone or other red crystal

1. On a sunny day just after the sun's move into Leo, take your crystal outside and place it in direct sunlight. Sit before the stone and affirm: 'This crystal will always remind me of the abundance of summer.'
2. Leave the stone in situ until the sun sets to imbue it with solar power.
3. Now take the crystal inside and place it centre stage on your altar or sacred table until the sun moves out of Leo (on around 22 August). Find a dedicated space to keep your summer stone, and when you feel you want to recall or reawaken the joyful experience of summer, hold it or wear it for as long as you desire.

MYTH

In Wiccan tradition, Ceridwen is the Welsh goddess of magic, wisdom, shape-shifting, rebirth and transformation. She possesses a cauldron filled with a magic elixir, known as *awen* (a gift of knowledge, creativity and poetic inspiration). In some Wiccan circles, it is believed that her festival falls on 3 July, so I have used this as the basis for her inclusion in this chapter.

In medieval Welsh legend, Ceridwen was an enchantress and mother of two children: an ugly son, Mordfran, and a beautiful daughter, Creirwy. One legend relays how Ceridwen wanted to bestow upon her son the gifts of the *awen*, so she ordered Gwion, a young boy-servant, to stir the elixir. As he did so, three drops spilled on to his thumb, and it was Gwion who gained the wisdom and knowledge that had been intended for Mordfran. In her fury, Ceridwen sought revenge, chasing Gwion through the skies and seas, before eventually killing the boy, who was later reborn to her as the Welsh bard, Taliesin.

TALIESIN

Poetry played a major part in Doreen Valiente's development of Wiccan ritual and practice (see page 3), and in Welsh legend, the semi-mythical bard Taliesin represents the power of poetic inspiration. Taliesin is said to have been a sixth-century poet who sang at the courts of at least three kings. During the medieval period, he was celebrated as a mythic hero, and was thought to have been a companion to King Arthur. An extant Welsh manuscript made up of fifty-six poems, known as *The Book of Taliesin,* dates from the fourteenth century CE, although many of the poems are believed to be much older. There are many verses about *awen* and its importance as a source of inspiration for bards and poets. The text also includes mysterious lines thought to be the words of an oracle, a divine voice, or a pathway to enable the reader/speaker to connect with the gods.

AWEN RITUAL

Why not use a little of Ceridwen's magical *awen* to revitalise and encourage creative thinking for a summer of happiness?

You will need:
a white tealight candle
a few drops of patchouli or rose essential oil (or just
    almond oil, if you're allergic to essential oils)
a bowl of still spring water
a handful of summer flower petals of your choice

1. Safely light the candle for atmosphere, then drizzle your chosen oil into the water and watch as the two separate.
2. As you do so, reflect on how this is your vessel of inspiration, swirling with intoxicating oils and purifying water.
3. Gradually drop some of the flower petals into the water and swirl them around with your finger. As you do so, say: 'Thank you, Ceridwen, for bringing your magic potion to me with summer inspiration for (add whatever creative act you'd like to invoke). Blessed be.'
4. Once you have made your statement, blow out the candle and leave your *awen* overnight to draw down Ceridwen's inspiration.
5. This simple ritual will encourage you to activate the very thing you desire, whether travelling, creating your masterpiece or trying out a new lifestyle.

WICCAN MYTH CYCLE

The Earth Goddess and Sun God have romanced at the equinox, danced at Beltane and completed their union at the summer solstice. Power is now slipping away from the Sun God, as his solar light begins to wane, and the Earth Goddess is pregnant with his power. The goddess knows that all that has been seeded will come to bear fruit, as she has transformed from Maiden to Mother. The power is in her hands, as she has the potential to generate a bountiful harvest, or a lean one.

FULL MOON: HAY MOON

'Make hay while the sun shines' is a familiar folklore adage that encourages us to take advantage of a good opportunity when one presents itself. It finds its roots in traditional farming, dating back to the early Celtic Iron Age period, when grass would be cut to make hay while it was still light outside. So it's hardly surprising that the July full moon became known as the Hay Moon (however, a full moon in the first week of July could be considered to be the nearest full moon to the summer solstice, and therefore it is sometimes called the Mead Moon – see page 105). In Celtic tradition, when hay was brought in from the fields, it was a time to rejoice and give thanks to both the Earth Goddess for the crop, and also to the lunar goddess (Rhiannon is traditionally favoured at this full moon) for her lunar energy. We may be more likely to associate gardening with solar energy, but many Wiccans continue the gardening tradition of using the phases of the moon for planting, reaping, sowing, weeding and so on.

MAKE HAY WHILE THE SUN SHINES

This July full moon, why not do a little ritual 'haymaking' to help you enjoy the spirit of summer and give thanks to the goddesses for their summer blessings?

1. Either just before, or on the day of the full moon, set out for your experience. Find an green open space, such as a field, a garden, or any grassy spot.
2. When you reach your chosen location, sit down

and gently take a handful of grass in each hand, without picking it. You could even lie on your back if the ground is dry enough. Rub your hands lightly back and forth over the grass and be aware of the sensations that it gives you. Is the grass soft, gentle, cool, refreshing? What experiences and feelings come to you? If you were to cut it now, how would you make hay from it?

3. Break off a handful of grass (it won't mind; in fact; this will make it grow even stronger). Hold it out before you as an offering to both goddesses and say: 'With this hay, I can make my own sunshine. Thank you for your blessings.' Sprinkle the grass freely before you.

4. After this ritual, if any opportunity comes your way, remember to 'make hay while the sun shines', and give thanks to both goddesses for their guidance.

CONNECT TO NATURE

Beech tree nuts ripen as the leaves darken, and these magnificent trees offer welcome shade for wildlife and wandering Wiccans alike on any hot July day. Decked in their finery of beautifully scented cream flowers, statuesque lime trees buzz with hundreds of bees. Young swallows and swifts take to the air, and we may be lucky to spot a rare hummingbird hawk moth hovering beside a garden petunia to collect nectar.

The start of July can sometimes be cloudy, rainy and not

much like the idyll of summer we imagine it to be – but as trees flourish above, their canopy of leaves shelters all that lies beneath them, and there is something quite mystical about a rainy woodland grove on a summer's day.

In traditional Wicca, the sacred grove is a secret place for a coven to perform magical rites, with its whereabouts known only to the initiates. Sacred groves are usually found in woodland, and can be formed of a natural copse or small circle of trees. Since ancient times, they have been associated with deities or spirits, and have long been sites for ritual and worship.

SACRED GROVE RITUAL

If you're lucky enough to live near a forest or woodland, then you can choose and sanctify your own grove. If not, choose a tree nearby with which you feel an affinity and treat it as a familiar, sacred tree that will protect and stand by you.

1. To encourage a connection to the spirit of the place, stand in your grove, wood or beneath your tree, then reach your arms up to the sky and gaze upwards.
2. Take a few slow, deep breaths to imbue you with the energy of the trees around you, and to give your energy back to them. When you are centred and ready, lower your arms back down to your sides.
3. Touch one tree, and absorb the energy of its spiritual and physical presence for a moment or two. Try standing with your back close to the

trunk, with one hand behind your back, palm pressed against the tree, and one hand to your belly. Imagine you are breathing in the power of the tree, and giving back your gratitude with each breath.

4. Carry on like this for about a minute or so to feel empowered by your sacred grove. Then reach down for a stone, a leaf, a twig, or anything that catches your eye, and place it in the middle of your grove or beneath the tree to show your respect and honour for this place.

5. You will feel empowered and elated when you leave your sacred grove.

THE SACRED GROVE

The most famous sacred oak grove in ancient Greece was at Dodona, renowned for the oracle of Zeus and originally devoted to an ancient mother goddess, possibly Dione. Another sacred grove lay on the northern shore of Lake Nemi in Italy, home of the sanctuary of the Italic goddess, Diana Nemorensis, 'Diana of the Wood', who was later identified with the Roman goddess Diana. Vesta, the Roman goddess of the hearth and home, was also worshipped in the grove at Nemi. The Celtic word *nemeton* means 'a sacred natural site', and Nemotona was the Celtic goddess of the grove.

The first-century CE Roman naturalist Pliny wrote that Druids performed all their religious rites in oak groves, gathering mistletoe from the trees with a golden sickle (see page 210 to learn more about mistletoe in oak trees).

STARLORE

July is best known for the appearance of three exceptionally bright stars that make a clear triangle in the night sky: an asterism known as the Summer Triangle. It is made up of Vega, Altair and Deneb. Vega, the fifth-brightest star visible from Earth, and part of the small constellation of Lyra, sits 'on top' of the Summer Triangle from our vantage point in the northern hemisphere. Deneb, the brightest star in Cygnus, marking the tail of the 'swan constellation', is the western point of the triangle. Altair, the twelfth-brightest star in our sky, marks the eastern point, and is part of the constellation Aquila. To spot this magnificent triangle, look towards the east late at night (from the UK), and the three bright stars will stand out prominently against the backdrop of the mystical, shimmering galaxy known as the Milky Way.

On a moonless July night, when the sky is clear, locate the Summer Triangle and reflect on how these three stars unite the constellations across the Milky Way. In the same way, July is a uniting force between the fertility festivals of Beltane and the summer solstice, and the harvest festivals to come, reminding us that they are inseparable and part of the ongoing cycle of the Wheel of the Year.

TAROT: STRENGTH

Like the fire sign of Leo, Strength reminds us of our inner courage, and our ability to face challenges and to keep going in the face of difficulty. In fact, whenever you draw this card, it tells you that in order to move forward successfully, you need the qualities of compassion aligned with self-esteem, and tenacity aligned with gentle persuasion, plus authenticity and belief in yourself. Draw this card and place it on your altar or sacred space from about 21 July until 20 August to align with the empowering influence of the sun in Leo. It will encourage you to take responsibility for your actions and choices.

AUGUST

'That which is below is like that which is above,
and that which is above is like that which is below.'

The Emerald Tablet,
translated by ISAAC NEWTON

AUGUST AT A GLANCE

THEMES	harvest, boldness, discernment
FESTIVAL/FOCUS	Lammas/Lughnasadh
DEITY	Opis
CRYSTALS	sunstone/peridot
ELEMENTS	fire/earth
FULL MOON	Grain/Corn Moon
TREE	oak
BIRD	swallow
PLANT	sunflower
ZODIAC	Leo/Virgo
TAROT	the Hermit

SEASON AND CYCLE

In the Celtic agricultural calendar, August is the month of the first harvest. According to some historians, August was named after the Emperor Augustus, marking some of his major conquests. Others have suggested that the name derives from *augurs*, oracular priests and priestesses who interpreted the behaviour of birds as messages from the gods to divine the future. Although bird activity still seems quiet in August, young swallows, house martins and swifts are busily feeding, growing stronger and preparing for their autumn migration to hotter climes.

Acorns are nearly ripe, and the oak tree proudly displays its green finery, outclassing other trees, such as elder, birch and lime, which begin to look a little tarnished at the edges. Birdsong (apart from the 'hoo-hoos' of wood pigeons and collared doves) is rarely heard, as our feathered friends shield from predators as best they can during their moulting period. This is a month of extremes, from the rampant growth of berries and bindweed to the slowly maturing sloes in the hedgerows. The waning sun, although torrid and hot at times, reminds us that autumn is not far off as it sinks lower in the sky. This last month of summer is an opportunity to be bold, to enjoy a little opulence, and to reflect on what we have accomplished so far this year.

THE MIGHTY OAK

The oak holds on to its beautiful leaves well into the beginning of winter, one of the signs of its strength and endurance. In Druid lore, the oak was prized for its healing and magical powers. In British folk tradition, it was believed that if you walked around an oak tree as you made a wish, that wish would come true if a bird alighted on the branches before you departed. A nail driven into an oak tree was thought to cure toothache, while rubbing the oak's trunk with your left hand on Midsummer's Day would keep you healthy all year.

CELEBRATING AUGUST

FESTIVAL: LUGHNASADH/LAMMAS

The first day of August marks the Celtic festival of Lughnasadh, and the beginning of the harvest season. The day is more commonly known as the Christian celebration of Lammas (meaning 'loaf mass'), when loaves of bread made from the first wheat crop were brought to church to be blessed. For Wiccans, this sabbat also marks the important midpoint between the summer solstice and the autumn equinox in the Wheel of the Year, and honours the first 'real' harvest of the summer.

Lughnasadh is named after the Celtic god Lugh, identified as a warrior and king, and sometimes a solar deity. He was skilled in many arts, including spear-throwing and magic, and was one of the Tuatha Dé Danann, the first supernatural beings of Irish mythology. There are many legends and myths about him and the origins of his festival. One suggests that Lughnasadh was a celebration of Lugh's triumph over a malevolent god (known in Irish folklore as Crom Dubh) in a battle over the first harvested grain crops. Crom Dubh wanted to keep it all to himself, while Lugh wished to share it with all mankind.

One of the earliest Lughnasadh festivals took place at Tailteann (Teltown in County Meath). The Tailteann Games, thought to date back as far as 1600 BCE, were said to have been founded by Lugh in memory of his foster-mother, the earth goddess Tailtiu, who died after clearing all the lands of Ireland for mankind to farm. With Christianisation, the games were phased out, but were revived during the medieval period at the Tailtin Fair, which consisted of contests of strength and skill, horse races, dancing and handfasting ceremonies.

According to various Irish folklore accounts, Lughnasadh festivities vary depending on the region, but most rituals included offering Lugh the first ears of corn, which were placed on a high hilltop to represent his strength, and then buried to represent his waning power. It was also believed that Lugh's life-giving power was transferred to the grain, and that once the grain was harvested, Lugh then descended into the darkness until the following spring. A feast followed, including the meat of a sacrificial bull and the first fruit of the season, usually bilberries. And, of course, there was drinking, dancing, music and games.

A number of fairs are believed to have once been associated with the celebration of Lughnasadh; for example, the Puck Fair at Killorglin, County Kerry. Wiccans usually celebrate this day by joining with others for a special feast, or making a pilgrimage to a mountain or their highest local hill to honour Lugh.

LUGHNASADH FEASTING

To make this day special, you can celebrate by arranging a feast that gives thanks to your preferred deities. You may want to honour Lugh himself, and his foster-mother Tailtiu, or you may choose to honour the Sun God and Earth Goddess. Whoever you choose, here are some ideas that you might like to incorporate to enhance and encourage the goodness of the harvest:

- Bake or purchase a delicious loaf of bread as a symbolic offering of the first ears of wheat.
- Decorate your dining table with seasonal flowers, herbs and anything that you can use as motifs for the first harvest. I like to use a bunch of seasonal flowers, such as marigolds or sunflowers, a selection of seasonal herbs, such as vervain, marshmallow, basil and oregano, ears of wheat, corn dollies, gold crystals such as sunstone or goldstone, and gold or orange candles to energise your home with the abundant energy of the harvest.

- As part of the ritual, make a toast to the deities of your choice with your favourite drink, then break the loaf with your hands and share it with friends or family, whether they are in your company or not. If they are not physically present, place portions of bread around your table as if they were. For those who are present, share your favourite meal together or just enjoy the day.

CREATIVE WISDOM RITUAL

August is not only a time to celebrate the abundance of the first harvest, it's also a month to encourage creativity in all its forms. Lugh's foster-mother, the goddess Tailtiu, was an archetypal creatrix and an aspect of the Earth Goddess, giving life to the world and sacrificing herself in her toil and labour for humanity's benefit. This is a time to honour your skills and talents, to evolve, and to create new avenues for manifesting these skills. This ritual will imbue you with Tailtiu's gift of preparing the 'ground', ready for your own sowing and reaping to come.

You will need:
a sunstone or other gold-coloured stone (for creativity)
a piece of peridot (for wisdom and Tailtiu)
60 cm (2 foot) length of gold-coloured ribbon or cord (for the Sun God)
a green tealight candle (for grounding ideas)

1. Place the two crystals on a flat surface and wind the gold ribbon around them to make a circle of protection. As you do so, affirm: 'Thank you both, Sun God and Earth Goddess, Tailtiu, for your gifts of nature.'

2. Light the tealight candle and place it in front of the circle to amplify creative power. Now say, 'With these stones, I will grow in creative strength and wisdom. Thank you, Sun God and Earth Goddess, Tailtiu for the creative harvest that I too will reap. Blessed be.'

3. Now blow out the candle to seal your petition to the deities. Keep the gold circle on your altar until the end of August to empower you with creative ideas, confidence and determination to succeed.

SUNSTONE AND PERIDOT

The two zodiac signs of August, fire sign Leo and earth sign Virgo, are associated with sunstone and peridot respectively. Sunstone encourages enthusiasm, courage, self-awareness and strength of character, while peridot offers clarity, logic, consideration and discernment. Using these two crystals in any ritual will invoke the elements of fire and earth, a powerful combination for making progress. Without the spark of creative genius, symbolised by the sunstone, the Sun

> God's illuminating power may become lost in the dark, while peridot's grounding influence means that the Earth Goddess can help you to manifest your goal.

A LUGHNASADH PILGRIMAGE

Making a pilgrimage to a hill or mountain is still a popular Wiccan way to honour the god Lugh. If you can't get to a hill, you can always just find a spot out there in nature where you feel in harmony with the world around you. This is where you will give gratitude not only to the god, but also to yourself and the universe. Try this short gratitude pilgrimage at any time during the month of August.

You will need:
a piece of paper and a pen
an offering for the season (perhaps a sheaf of wheat, a small bunch of seasonal flowers, or a small loaf of bread)

1. When you arrive at your destination, find a quiet spot to sit and reflect. Relax for a few moments, thank Lugh for his blessing, and then ask yourself: 'What seeds have I sown for my future intentions since Imbolc, if any?'

2. If you haven't 'sown any seeds,' write about how that makes you feel. Perhaps you'll write: 'I don't have to prove anything to anyone, not even myself;

if I truly believe in myself, then it is enough to be true to who I am.'

3. If you have made progress or achieved anything you set out to do, however big or small, write down the work you have done. Even thinking about doing so is enough to show your commitment to yourself, and to know that you can continue to make progress as the year unfolds.

4. Finally, write: 'I am grateful for all that I do and will do. Blessed be.'

5. Fold up your paper and, if you like, write 'Lughnasadh gratitude' on the outside to seal your intention. Now bury the paper in the soil, or push it into the undergrowth where it will eventually disintegrate. Place your petition of flowers or wheat on top of where you have buried the paper and say: 'I give thanks at Lughnasadh for this pilgrimage to honour Lugh and also myself, and know that what I have achieved and what I can harvest in the months to come is for the good of All.'

6. Leave your spot and make your way back home, knowing that you have, like Lugh, shared your 'harvest' with everything and everyone, including yourself.

MYTH

There are many goddesses worldwide identified with the harvest, including the Sabine (ancient people of central Italy) and Roman goddess of abundance, Opis. Opis, meaning 'plenty', was the wife of the Roman god Saturn (their equivalents in Greek mythology are Rhea and Cronus). In artistic works, Opis is usually depicted holding a sheaf of corn or sometimes a cornucopia. Like Rhea, Opis was originally an ancient chthonic (underworld) earth goddess, who gave life to that which 'grew' below ground rather than merely above (this included crystals, underground springs, and so on). During the month of August, there were two harvest festivals for Opis. The first was on 10 August, and the second, known as the Opiconsivia, was usually held on 25 August. There are few stories about Opis herself, but her daughter Ceres, the bountiful and loving goddess of the grain, could, if wronged, withhold all growth on Earth – or, as in one story, inflict personal hunger on an individual. Erysichthon, the prince of Thessaly, felled one of Ceres's sacred trees, even when the spirit of the tree wailed in pain at the first swing of his axe. Angered by his disrespect, Ceres cursed Erysichthon with insatiable hunger. After spending all his wealth to buy food, he eventually devoured himself. This shows that while harvest deities may indeed give, they can just as easily take.

RITUAL TO BASK IN THE OPULENCE OF OPIS AND CERES

Opis and her daughter Ceres ask you to harvest your own goodness, rather than take from others. If you abide by this, you will attract a little opulence or opportunity into your life at this time of year. Here's how.

You will need:

2 handfuls of wholegrains (such as wheat, barley or rye)

1. Find a peaceful spot in nature where you can invoke and give thanks to Opis and Ceres. To channel their blessing, first petition Opis. As she dwells beneath the earth, you need to make direct contact with the soil. Gently push one handful of grain deep into the ground to affirm your connection to the goddess.
2. As you do so, say: 'Opis, bless me with the spirit of opportunity, and I will return only goodness and goodwill to all the Earth, both below and above.'
3. Now, to be blessed by Ceres, take the other handful of grain and cast it before you across the ground. As you do so, say, 'Ceres, bless me with fertile ideas, so I may give all my goodness back to the Earth, both below and above. Blessed be.'

WICCAN MYTH CYCLE

As the summer progresses, the Sun God's light lessens a little each day, and although his heat can still burn our skin and scorch the earth, he sinks lower towards the horizon, knowing that soon he will return to the underworld, where he will await his rebirth at the winter solstice. He has devoted all his power to generating abundance for the Earth Goddess, who, impregnated with his seed, draws on his power to amplify her own.

FULL MOON: GRAIN/CORN MOON

In Celtic tradition, the August full moon is known as the Grain Moon or Corn Moon, due to its association with the first harvest.

The Grain Moon invites us to reflect on not only Lugh's power to vitalise the corn, but also the full moon aspect of the Triple Goddess symbol. As we have seen, the full moon, or Mother phase, represents ripeness, fulfilment, fertility and power. In the Wheel of the Year, it is associated with the summer solstice, the harvest of Lughnasadh and the autumn equinox. The Crone phase is associated with the waning moon and dark of the moon phase. The Crone symbolises wisdom, life experience, secret knowledge and mystery, and accepting that the only constant in life is change itself. In the Wheel of the Year, the Crone is associated with Samhain and Yule. The Maiden phase is symbolic not only of the waxing moon but also the growing period of early spring, and symbolises enchantment, birth and beginnings. So the Maiden phase in the the Wheel of the Year corresponds to Imbolc, the spring equinox and Beltane.

So, this August full moon, why not reflect on the Mother phase of the cycle and think about how this energy might appear in your own life? What does the harvest mean to you? Can you relate to the ideas of the Mother and 'fullness', and the reaping of your own talents?

It may seem that there are quite a few questions to ask yourself this month, but August is the perfect month for self-reflection, as it's influenced by Leo's concerns with self and Virgo's with clarification.

DEMETER, CORN MOTHER

In Greek mythology, Demeter was the goddess of the harvest and the grain, who sustained humanity with the earth's rich bounty. In Homer's *Iliad*, Demeter is described as sifting the chaff from the grain, presenting her as the goddess who shares out the fruits of the earth, rather than the goddess of planet Earth itself, the domain of her great-grandmother, Gaia. Demeter was also the mother of Persephone, the wife of Hades. Distraught at Hades's abduction of her daughter, Demeter neglected the earth, and in her despair, all crops ceased to grow. Concerned by the growing cries of the starving and pressure from other deities, Zeus persuaded Hades to let Persephone return to the upper world in order to appease Demeter. For six months each year, from the first signs of spring until the end of the harvest season, Persephone was reunited with her mother. In classical art, Demeter is depicted holding a sheaf of corn or sometimes a cornucopia, while in early Greek iconography, she carries a poppy, an ancient symbol of abundant wild growth, and wears a headdress made of corn.

CONNECT TO NATURE

If you look very carefully among grassy banks, wild meadows or downland, you may come across some delightful secrets of nature, such as the tiny bird's-foot trefoil with its yellow flowers that, from a distance, look like miniature yellow polka dots in a sea of luscious green. August is the perfect month to observe as many wildflowers or plants as you can, as most are now in bloom. Take photos, draw or paint them, and remember that even the tiniest or most unassuming of flowers can encourage a diversity of wildlife and benefit the local ecosystem.

If you have space in your garden or a spare hanging flower pot, it's not too late to create a wild microcosm by sowing wildflower seeds that will appear in the autumn to attract late summer bees and other pollinating insects.

THE WILDSCAPE WHEEL

A traditional Wiccan way to engage with nature and encourage your sense of creativity is to spend a few days collecting foliage, flowers and other natural objects, such as twigs, stones, nuts, shells, pebbles and driftwood. Use these to create a wildscape wheel, which acts as a celebratory mandala of the first harvest. Please remember to be respectful when foraging for items, and avoid picking fresh blossoms and other thriving plant life.

1. On a smooth surface, create a rough circle with your chosen items.

2. Then start in the centre, and gradually create your wheel by working outwards, perhaps first creating eight spokes to represent the Wheel of the Year, then filling in the segments with patterns, abstract lines or whatever 'comes through' from your intuition. Sometimes, we instinctively know where a colour, item or design will be; at others, we may have to jiggle things around or start again, until we think, *Hey, this feels right!*

3. Enjoy the process, and remember to give this gift of your love of nature back to the source when finished, by saying: 'This wildscape wheel is in celebration of the abundance of Mother Earth at this time of year, and I thank you sun, moon, Earth and stars for this, and show my appreciation for all.'

STARLORE

Ursa Major, the Plough and the Summer Triangle are still visible in the night sky at this time, but perhaps the highlight of August is the sizzling display of shooting stars in the northern sky in the form of the Perseid meteor shower, which comes as the Earth moves through the debris of an ancient dead comet. Emanating from the constellation Perseus, the Perseids burn up in our atmosphere, creating one of the most spectacular displays of shooting stars of the year. Ancient superstition tells us that if you make a wish when you see a shooting star, it will come true. This is a great opportunity to make as many wishes as you like!

TAROT: THE HERMIT

We may like to consider reaping the benefits of our gifts and work so far this year, but the Hermit reminds us that we sometimes need to look back with insight, to wonder how we can be more discerning in the future, and to follow our own insights, rather than listening to other people's opinions. In fact, a little soul-searching and self-questioning will lead you to the right course of action for the months ahead. Consider placing this card on your altar or sacred space to remind you to trust your spirit guide, a chosen deity or your own intuition.

SEPTEMBER

'He found himself wondering at times, especially in the autumn, about the wild lands, and strange visions of mountains that he had never seen came into his dreams.'

J. R. R. TOLKIEN,
The Fellowship of the Ring

SEPTEMBER AT A GLANCE

THEMES	Preservation, preparation, transition, balance
FESTIVAL/FOCUS	the Autumn Equinox
DEITY	the Horned God
CRYSTALS	peridot/rose quartz
ELEMENTS	earth/air
FULL MOON	Harvest Moon
TREE	hazel
BIRD	sparrowhawk
PLANT	bramble
ZODIAC	Virgo/Libra
TAROT	Justice

SEASON AND CYCLE

September is rooted in the Latin word for seven, *septem*, as it was originally the seventh month of the old Roman calendar. The Anglo-Saxons referred to it as *gerst monath*, 'barley month', or *haefest monath*, 'harvest month', as it was a time for harvesting barley grain to make a popular alcoholic drink. For us, it is time to celebrate the second harvest of the year, the fruit harvest.

Early morning mists, apple-strewn lawns, and 'mellow fruitfulness', to borrow from Keats, capture the essence of September in the northern hemisphere. Due to our changing climate, it can often feel that autumn has shifted to October, but even if the summer weather carries on for longer than expected, the light in September is different, and the sun seems to begin to lose its heat. On clear nights, the chill air comes quickly, followed by a morning landscape bejewelled with dew. September and the equinox mark the transition between summer and winter, a time when we are filled with fruit and wine and contented, knowing that we must take what we can now, for the winter 'queen' is coming.

CELEBRATING SEPTEMBER

FESTIVAL: THE AUTUMN EQUINOX

The autumn equinox usually occurs between 21 and 24 September, and, like the spring equinox, gives us equal amounts of daylight and darkness across the world. The sun begins to slip over the equator, heading further south, and it's time to reap the rewards of our sunny spring and summertime ideas and prepare for winter.

In Wiccan circles, the name Mabon was first used to refer to the autumn equinox in the 1970s. It was given this name by prominent Wiccan practitioner and author Aidan Kelly, who, as we have seen, also named the spring equinox Ostara and the summer solstice Litha. All three names are controversial among most Wicca groups, and the terms 'solstice' and 'equinox' are preferred, but it is up to you which you use.

The autumn equinox is about giving thanks to the Earth Goddess as she provides us with her bounty, and to the Sun God for his gift of transferring his power to her. In ancient Greece, the autumn equinox marked the time when Persephone returned to the underworld to join her consort, Hades, for the six months of autumn and winter. Wiccans and modern pagans see the equinox as a time to celebrate the recent bounty of summer and its life-giving light, and to accept and welcome the darker days to come as we move towards the winter solstice and, later, the spring equinox. Yet autumn and winter bring their own joys. We can now experience the spirit of harvest time, and enjoy our own beacon of light that shows us the way forwards to the next turn of the Wheel at Samhain and beyond.

WHO IS MABON?

Mabon is derived from the name 'Mabon ap Modron', meaning 'divine son of the divine mother', a Welsh deity linked by Kelly with the arrival of autumn. The tale of Mabon is obscure, but recounts how he was snatched from his mother when he was a few days old, and imprisoned in an underwater dungeon for thousands of years until he was rescued by King Arthur's men in order to perform a heroic task. Kelly suggested that this myth echoed that of Persephone, who was snatched by Hades and taken to the underworld, leaving her mother, the fertility goddess Demeter, to grieve. As her mother's grief caused the loss of all growth on earth, it was agreed that Persephone would spend half the year (autumn equinox to spring equinox) with Hades, and the other half in the upper world with her mother. The rather tenuous link drawn by Kelly between Mabon's tale and Persephone's has cast much doubt in Wiccan circles about Kelly's renaming of the two equinoxes and the summer solstice.

As this is the last true festival of abundance, celebrate the mellow season with a feast, either with your friends, family or coven, or alone. To celebrate the autumn equinox, Wiccans usually offer their own harvested delights as a token of their gratitude, such as produce from the garden or crafts they have made. If you're not the gardening or crafty type, here's a simple way to create your own offering.

You will need:
a decorative bowl
a selection of fruit, nuts, herbs and spices
12 autumnal candles (in shades of ochre, yellow, orange, red and green)
a pastry or cake of your choice

1. Fill the decorative bowl with your selection of fruits, nuts, herbs and spices, then place it on a table with the pastry or cake next to it.
2. Form a festive ring around the bowl using the candles, before carefully lighting each one to seal your intention to the Sun God and Earth Goddess, and to invoke the energy of the harvest season.
3. Take a few moments to reflect on what the harvest means to you, and how blessed and thankful you are for the abundance in nature.
4. Now take pleasure in your own favourite meal or feast. At the end of your celebration, say the following prayer of gratitude:

'I thank the Earth Goddess and the Sun God for the gifts before us and all around us; I thank nature for its joy, whether the spirit of the rain, the snow, the breeze, the heat or the gale – all is welcome here to join in this celebration of the balance of night and day.'

BALANCING RITUAL

This equinox is a time to see that, despite the loss of summer, we can find beauty in the return of autumn and winter. Any regret that summer is gone is, in fact, an opportunity for gratitude; we can be thankful for what we have enjoyed, and be reminded of what will come around to us again.

On the day of the equinox, try this simple ritual to see the light in the darkness.

You will need:

a large selection of stones or pebbles (you will need these to
    create a spiral that you will walk along)
a piece of citrine (for clarity)
a white tealight candle (for light)
a black tealight candle (for dark)

1. Arrange the stones or pebbles into a spiral that is large enough to walk along. Start at the centre, and spiral the stones outwards in a clockwise direction. Place an unlit black candle at the centre of the spiral, and an unlit white candle at the end of

the spiral. (If you are careful and aware of safety, then you can choose to light both candles for more atmosphere.)

2. When you're focused and centred, pick up the white candle and the citrine, and slowly walk, following the spiral path's inwards. With each step, imagine you are walking into the centre of yourself.

3. When you reach the black candle, place the citrine next to it, then place the white candle on the other side of the citrine. Reflect on the balance that the candles represent: see how light is equal to dark. Imagine and feel this equilibrium within you, even just for a moment: an instant of knowing you are both light and dark, summer and winter. Hold this feeling for a moment longer, then let it go.

4. Leave your candles and crystal at the centre, and then walk the spiral back out, knowing you have experienced the balance of summer and winter within you. When you are ready, return to the centre, remove your crystal and candles, and leave your stones in place as a sign of your connection to the universe.

5. Resolve to recall the best moments of your spring and summer as winter arrives, and to see how, in the darkness, there is always a light shining within you. So let it shine!

THE FEAST OF AVALON RITUAL

The autumn equinox is also known in some Wiccan traditions as the Feast of Avalon – a reference to the mystical 'isle of apples' of Arthurian legend, a supernatural land of eternal bliss. It was at Avalon that the enchantress Morgan le Fey and her sisters healed Arthur and brought him back to life. The apple in Celtic mythology is a symbol of spiritual healing and wholeness, and represents knowledge, abundance and the fruiting of ideas. The ancient Celts often celebrated the equinox with an apple feast, which traditionally included bread, cakes, ales and cider – and, of course, the first apples of the season. The apple is also prized for its hidden inner symbol, the pentagram. Cut an apple in half, and you will see the five-pointed star, representing the elements, spirit, fire, earth, air and water.

Here's how to honour all the fruits of the equinox season, celebrate the spirit of the apple and feel connected to its mystical healing power. You can do this ritual at any time during September when you feel the moment is right, either alone or with your chosen companions.

You will need:

5 apples

5 red, orange or green tealight candles

a selection of bread, cake, ale, cider or any drink of your choice

1. Arrange the apples in the shape of a pentagram on your table. Beside each apple, carefully light a tealight candle.

2. Focus your eyes for a few moments on each apple in turn, and imagine the pentagrams hidden within, then gaze at the complete pentagram before you and call on the Earth Goddess for blessings, and for the abundance of your harvest feast.

3. You might say, 'I call on the Earth Goddess to bring goodness and grace to my table, and give thanks for the bounty of apples and of all fruit which will ripen to fullness, as I too shall do this harvest season.'

4. Enjoy your feast, and as you celebrate the feast of Avalon, send out positive healing energy to not only those loved ones close to you, but for the good of All.

A TRIBUTE TO THE EARTH GODDESS

This is a ritual for when you have a couple of hours to spare, as you will need to visit an area of natural beauty. The intention is to forage for things that you can use to create a sacred autumnal tribute to the Earth Goddess to invoke harmonious energy. This is not an exhaustive list, but I would suggest looking out for the following:

sycamore seed pods ('keys' or 'helicopters') (for happy travels)
conkers (for strength)

hawthorn berries (for abundance)
rosehips, or any other wild seeds (for love, receiving and
    giving)
wild stones or pebbles (for grounding)
hazelnuts (for wisdom)

1. When you are home from your foraging trip, place
    your chosen votives in a decorative bowl and dis-
    play the bowl in a prominent place in your home
    to attract positivity for you, your home and your
    family.
2. As you do so, say, 'Thank you, Earth Goddess, for
    bounty and abundance, and for bringing harmony
    to my home. Blessed be.'

WELCOME THE WINTER

In the six weeks before Samhain, we are busy harvesting,
and we can indulge in giving and receiving, preserving
and preparation. Then, between Samhain and the winter
solstice, we can fill the darker days by delighting in the
landscape. With a different perspective, we can appreciate
the beauty of the stark trees and the changing weather,
from stormy gales to crisp, clear days. All these moments
are enriching. This is a time to take pleasure in slowing
down and to begin preparing ourselves for winter solstice
festivities. We can feel revived by the knowledge that soon
the Sun God will be reborn, and we too will experience a
feeling of regrowth.

HAZEL TREE MAGIC

In many mythologies, the hazel tree was the sacred tree of wisdom. In Celtic legend, at the centre of the Otherworld (the supernatural realm of deities), nine magic hazel trees dropped their nuts into the Well of Wisdom. From this well, the nuts were carried downstream, and any bird, animal, mortal or spirit who ate the nuts would be filled with prophetic wisdom. In folklore, hazel rods protect against evil spirits and are used for water-divining, while the nuts were carried as amulets to ward off rheumatism, and were also used in divination. In a poem titled, 'The Shepherd's Week: Thursday; Or, The Spell', by eighteenth-century English poet John Gay, hazelnuts are used to divine true love:

> Two hazel nuts I threw into the flame,
> And to each nut I gave a sweetheart's name.
> This, with the loudest bounce me sore
>   amazed,
> That, with a flame of brightest colour
>   blazed.
> As blazed the nut, so may thy passion grow,
> For 'twas thy nut that did so brightly glow.

MYTH

Although this is primarily a time to celebrate the harvest, September was also associated with the nature gods of the wild woods and the hunt, including the Wiccan Horned God, and other horned gods such as Cernunnos, Ammon and Pan. In traditional Wicca, the Horned God is regarded as a dualistic god symbolising light and dark, night and day, summer and winter, as well as the Oak and Holly Kings (see page 96). Meanwhile, the Druids honoured the god of the forest, leaving offerings of harvested herbs, cider or fruit wine under oak trees. In some Wiccan traditions, he is also associated with a Triple God made up of Youth (Warrior), Father and Sage, corresponding to the Triple Goddess aspects of Maiden, Mother and Crone.

WILD WITHIN RITUAL

To honour all the gods of the wild and the autumn hunt, here is a ritual to draw on their powers and to remind you there is a wild spirit within you, too.

You will need:
a large piece of paper and a pen
2 green tealight candles
2 green crystals of your choice (such as green tourmaline or malachite)

1. Draw the symbol of the Horned God (see page 8) on a large sheet of paper. Place the two crystals in

the points of his horns, then light the tealights and place them above the points.

2. Focus on the image for a few moments, then close your eyes and visualise yourself journeying into a forest to meet the god.

3. All around you, the leaves are beginning to fall, the wind begins to blow and the light grows dim. Yet in a clearing, you glimpse movement. You sense a presence. Now open your eyes and look into the flame of one of the candles. Imagine it is the 'god of the forest' whom you are meeting. He holds out two green crystals to you, welcoming you to his realm.

4. Take up the two crystals before you and hold them close to your belly, saying: 'Thanks be to the god of the forest. With wild crystals at my side, I am potent, alive, protected in the forest of life. Blessed be.'

5. When you feel intuitively ready, blow out the candles to seal your intention to the god of the forest, and keep your crystals in a safe but prominent place to remind you that the wild spirit within you is as sacred as the compassion you have for all of the wild in nature.

WICCAN MYTH CYCLE

The Sun God's fertility is declining fast, and he is ready to descend to the dark land to be reborn at the winter solstice.

The Earth Goddess is bountiful, generous, fruitful, and she too prepares for the great change to come. There is a wistfulness about her now, a sadness for the loss of her lover into the darkness and the wild woods of the autumn, but she knows they will meet again in the spring on the ever-turning Wheel of the Year.

FULL MOON: HARVEST MOON

The Harvest Moon is traditionally the full moon closest to the equinox, so it may also fall in the first week of October. In Celtic tradition, it is sometimes known as the 'Barley Moon'. As with any full moon, this is a time when our intuition and wisdom are heightened, so it's a perfect opportunity to engage in some divination. Below, I've devised a simple Tarot spread reading that will invite you to consider what needs to be harvested, seeded and left to mulch down in your life.

TAROT READING FOR THE HARVEST MOON

1. Shuffle the cards and then lay them face down in a line across your table or altar. Run your finger slowly along the line of cards, back and forth for as long as you like, until you intuitively feel the moment is right to stop at a certain card.
2. Draw the first card for what can be 'left to mulch' on the ground.
3. Draw a second card for what needs to be seeded for future rewards.

4. Draw a final card to describe the outcome, and the bumper harvest to follow! (If you are not used to interpreting tarot cards, you can always look online for guidance.)

CONNECT TO NATURE

There's a fuss and commotion in the bushes and hedges, as flocks of tits (great tits, blue tits and sometimes coal and long-tailed tits) join forces. Safety in numbers protects them from predatory young sparrowhawks, who are now keeping a close look out for their lunch. Spiderwebs appear dew-draped in the morning. Tiny, almost invisible spiders parachute at impossible angles through the air in an attempt to land somewhere safe before a dashing young swallow catches them mid-leap. In the evening, awkward crane flies (daddy-long-legs) bump haphazardly against our windows, before they take their final bow after a short life on the world stage.

ADMIRE A FAIRY RING

September is also the time of year when, as if by magic, rings of mushrooms appear in forests, woods and damp, grassy places. Unless you are a very experienced forager, I don't recommend gathering fungi, but that doesn't mean you can't engage with this amazing creation of nature in another way. Look out for these so-called fairy rings (also known as elf circles or pixie rings) on garden lawns, and in parks and shady woodlands.

There are many folk legends surrounding these rings, with most agreeing that they are caused by the magical energy of fairies or elves dancing in circles. In Welsh folklore, the fairies may lure you into their dance by enchanting you with their music, and one tale warns that if you step inside a fairy ring, you will have to dance forever with the fairy folk.

Rather than step inside a fairy ring and risk being whisked away by the little folk, why not just take a moment to admire this amazing creation of nature? And perhaps you would like to take part in a more positive folklore super-stition from England, which says that all you need to do is sit or stand beside the ring the first time it appears, and count the mushrooms. Whatever number you arrive at is the number of days (or some say weeks) until something wondrous will happen in your life. So why not try out a little fairy ring magic?

STARLORE

The constellation Pegasus, the winged horse, begins to dom-inate the evening sky in September. It can be easily spotted by looking for the four stars that mark out a square. This square is often used as a test of visibility by sky-watchers. The more stars you can see within the square, the better the atmospheric conditions for viewing the night sky. In Greek mythology, the winged horse Pegasus was captured by the Greek hero Bellerophon near the Pierian spring, with the help of Athena's golden bridle. The wild stallion allowed Bellerophon to ride him to defeat the monster Chimera, and the plucky horse went on to perform many more exploits with the hero.

This constellation reminds us that our wild, carefree spirit and our committed, civilised mindset can work together if we respect both these gifts.

TAROT: JUSTICE

Astronomically, the autumn equinox is the moment when the sun moves into the zodiac sign of Libra. The qualities associated with Libra are symbolised by the Justice card. This card tells us that objective thinking is needed if we are to find harmony. It reflects the theme of September's equinox, when we can see with a balanced perspective that all that we've done, and all that we hope to do, align perfectly with what we know to be our true intentions. This card also lets us know that it's time to accept that other people's sense of fair play may not be the same as ours. Leave this card on your sacred table or altar as a reminder of September's themes of fairness and equality in all aspects of your life.

OCTOBER

'Delicious autumn! My very soul is wedded to it,
and if I were a bird I would fly about the earth
seeking the successive autumns.'

GEORGE ELIOT,
letter to Miss Lewis, 1 October 1841

OCTOBER AT A GLANCE

THEMES	release, letting go, surrender, trust
FESTIVAL/FOCUS	start of Samhain (31 October)
DEITY	Hecate
CRYSTALS	black tourmaline/obsidian
ELEMENTS	air/water
FULL MOON	Hunter's/Blood Moon
TREE	blackthorn
BIRD	owl
PLANT	fly agaric (fungi)
ZODIAC	Libra/Scorpio
TAROT	the Empress

OCT

SEASON AND CYCLE

This is the month of the first windfall, leaf-fall, and acorn-fall. Similarly, it is the month when we fall into the realisation that we are losing a lot more light every day as we head towards the winter solstice. It may sound like an eternal gloomy descent into darkness for those who thrive in the sun. But we can also fall on to the sofa and allow ourselves to rest, or fall into someone's arms and allow ourselves to be loved, or even fall under the spell of caring for our deeper selves, using this time to surrender to the darkening days until the solstice lightens our spirits again.

If we look around us with eyes not blinded by the light of high summer, we can see that the changing season has its own beauty. We begin to see new, earthy autumnal landscapes that are soft and muted in the changing light. We can find this muted beauty in our own sensibility, if we allow ourselves to go with the essence of autumn for a while. So trust in how nature deals with the coming winter by closing in, settling down, and letting go of those things which no longer matter to you.

For some Wiccans, October marks the last month of the year (in keeping with the traditional Celtic agricultural year). This is the period of the 'blood harvest', when, traditionally, the last fruits were gathered, and livestock were brought into winter shelters or culled for food. Across the chilly valleys, the sound of wood being chopped could be heard in preparation for winter fires and the long, dark days ahead. Samhain traditionally falls across 31 October and 1 November, and the eve of Samhain marks an important and empowering point on the turning Wheel, which we celebrate in October.

CELEBRATING OCTOBER

FESTIVAL: SAMHAIN

Samhain (pronounced 'sa-wain' or 'sow-wain', meaning 'summer's end') was a Celtic celebration to mark the ending of the agricultural year and the beginning of the new one. Like most pagan peoples, the ancient Celts both feared and honoured their dead. This transition from the death of the old year to the birth of a new one was a time to 'meet the ancestors'. Samhain is thought to be a night when the boundary between the spirit and mundane world is no longer defined. We can begin to glimpse the numinous, and the spirit world can come close to us, if we let it. For the ancient Celts, it was particularly death, in its many guises (both sacred and sacrificial), that was at the core of this festival.

A time of both culling and preservation, much of the livestock was slaughtered at Samhain to be preserved as food supplies for the winter. Festivities lasted over several days, and involved the lighting of a communal bonfire or 'bone-fire', which included the bones and remains of slaughtered livestock. This not only served to honour the death of prized livestock, but also called on the ancestral dead for protection during the coming winter. All household fires were extinguished and then relit from the main bonfire with flaming torches brought to the home by one family member. Fires were left to burn all night in the hearth to welcome the ancestral spirits. Offerings of food were left out on tables to propitiate the ancestors and ensure their protection for the winter months. Samhain later reworked into Christian religion as All Hallows' Eve on 31 October, All Saints' Day or All Hallows' Day on 1 November and, some say, All Souls' Day on 2 November.

WICCAN SAMHAIN

For traditional Wiccans, Samhain is a time to cut away that which is no longer of importance, and to preserve that which is. It is also a time to acknowledge the eternal cycle of life and death. A traditional Wiccan Samhain evening usually consists of a ceremonial ritual to honour and remember the dead. Some traditional covens form a circle holding hands, and the High Priestess calls on the four directions and chosen deities for protection and blessing. Each member may name a loved one they have lost, or an ancestor for whom they have respect. Participants also reflect on their own past and the future, and the cycle of life, death and rebirth. Finally, the group gives thanks to the deities and asks for the ancestors' protection.

Sometimes, a 'dumb supper' is performed. This is a simple feast which can also be held among a coven, or friends or family. A place is set at the table to honour the dead, and the meal is held in total silence in reverence for the departed, and to give the spirits of the ancestors a time to 'contact' individuals through psychic or spiritual means, if so required.

SAMHAIN DECORATIONS

Decorate your altar or sacred space with produce that is in season, such as apples, pumpkins and gourds, to honour your ancestors and the traditions of the past. This simple act will align you with this deeply felt time of year, reminding you that endings are only natural and not something to fear, and that there are so many bright and beautiful things yet to come.

A SAMHAIN RITUAL

On Samhain Eve, we invite the spirits of past, present or future into our home to give us their protection. By connecting with and celebrating the spiritual world of your ancestors, you will be encouraged to feel a deeper connection to the spirit world.

If you are a Wiccan who practises witchcraft, Samhain is also the perfect time to call on any spirit entities you prefer to help manifest your goals or enhance personal power. In Doreen Valiente's (see page 3) version of the Wiccan Rede (the ethical code for Wiccans), she says:

> *'Cast the circle thrice about to keep the evil*
> *spirits out.*
> *To bind the spell every time let the spell be spake*
> *in rhyme.'*

Here is a ritual that embraces Doreen's approach. You can use it as a basis for any spells you want to create, or any that are already prescribed, but in this version of the ritual, I will show you how to call on the spirit world (often just known as 'spirit') to encourage a sense of self-empowerment.

You will need:
5 white tealight candles
5 red tealight candles
a mirror
5 oak leaves

1. Prop up the mirror on your altar or sacred space, and place the five white tealights in a pentagram shape before it, with each tealight representing a point of the star.
2. Arrange the five red tealights around the pentagram in an outer circle, then arrange the five oak leaves in a larger circle outside that.
3. Before you light the candles, cast a circle three times around you, and call in the four directions to protect you from any unwanted or negative spirit energy.
4. Hold out your arm to the east, and say, 'Thank you for your protection. Blessed be.' Say this for each of the other three directions, moving in a sunwise direction (east, south, west, north). Repeat this ritual circle twice more. You are now protected.
5. Relax and sit before your mirror and candles. Carefully light each candle, starting with the

furthest and finishing with the nearest for safety.

6. When all candles are lit, gaze into the mirror at the flames and let your eyes rest on the flickering lights. Imagine you are welcoming the spirits to you through these reflections.

7. As you do so, say:

> *'Kind souls unseen now come to me*
> *Your goodness shines this light to see*
> *Through this glass darkly, leaf and bough*
> *Bless me with wild and gentle power.'*

8. Continue to gaze into your mirror for as long as you feel is right for you, then thank the spirits for blessing and enhancing your own personal power.

9. Snuff out the candles carefully to release spirit from your sacred space. You will feel empowered in both mind and soul.

AUTUMNAL OAK RITUAL

Take care when walking under oak trees at this time of year, especially if it's windy, as you may find a whole family of acorns drops on your head at once! This bountiful tree sheds its children in large numbers, often all in one go, perhaps knowing only a few will survive to root and grow into magnificence. In most pagan beliefs, the oak is associated with strength, vitality, longevity and wisdom, and the acorn is also a symbol of growth and unlimited potential. It can take months or even a year for an acorn to sprout, and its dormant state reminds us that we too need periods of rest before we can grow in earnest.

1. When you next find yourself in an area with plenty of acorns, gather as many as you can and use them to form a circle on the ground that is big enough for you to step inside.

2. Step inside the circle and raise your arms outwards and upwards, reaching towards the sky like the branches of the oak tree. As you do so, say, 'I live like the oak with the seasons, and go with the flow of the cycle of growth. My own potential will flourish once I have rested awhile.'

3. Step outside of the circle, and then choose one acorn to take home with you. Keep it safe to show your trust in the magnanimity and power of the acorn, and to remind you that your own potential, when nurtured, is limitless.

OCTOBER TAROT CARD REFLECTION

October is a month for self-reflection, so use this simple divination exercise to consider your future.

You will need:
a white tealight candle
a mirror
a set of Tarot cards

1. Light the tealight candle and place it before the mirror. Shuffle the cards and lay them out in a long line, face down, in front of the candle and mirror.
2. Find inner stillness and relax for a moment, then look into the mirror and ask yourself, 'What potential can I develop in the months to come?' Study your reflection in the mirror – what do you see?
3. Now run your finger back and forth along the cards while you repeat the same question. When you feel the moment is right, stop, pick a card and place it face down in front of you.
4. Turn the card face up. This is another mirror, but this mirror never deceives or jests, and always tells the truth. In fact, the Tarot is a mirror of all that you are, and the card that you have picked has revealed to you the potential you can develop right now.

MYTH

The third aspect of the Triple Goddess, aligning with the dark of the new moon phase, is believed to be represented by Hecate, a chtonic (underworld) Greek goddess and accompanied by wild dogs, serpents, ghosts and owls. She was depicted carrying a burning torch, and was also associated with crossroads, sorcery, doorways and the wisdom of the Crone (see also November). During the dark of the new moon phase, a festive meal known as the Deipnon was dedicated to Hecate, and offerings were made to her entourage of restless spirits. These votives were left either on an altar, at a three-way crossroads, or at an intersection of the elements of air, water and earth – for example, on a rock jutting out of a river, or a bridge over a stream or pond. Hecate's flaming torches lit the pathway in the underworld when she and Demeter were searching for Demeter's daughter, Persephone, and similarly, during Samhain, she lights up the dark pathways of the spirit world, and also provides a light to help us to make our way safely through the dark of winter. If you celebrate Hecate's power, she can lead you along the right pathway for inspiration for the months ahead.

HECATE'S INSPIRATION RITUAL

1. During the dark of the new moon phase in October, lay out fruit, nuts or any plants you may have foraged on your altar as an offering to Hecate to empower you with her wisdom.
2. Leave the offering for two nights, then remove it. You will begin to sense her inspirational presence, knowing that she is by your side.

HECATE'S SLOE GIN

The blackthorn tree has long been associated with Hecate. Blackthorns are fruiting trees, and in October their sloe berries are ripe and ready to pick, and can be used to make sloe gin. So why not harvest the blackthorn's dark berries (this is best done after the first frost), and make a little of this wintry alcoholic drink as a gesture of appreciation to the goddess? After all, without the darkness, we would not appreciate the light. Hecate lights the way in the underworld, so honour her attributes and be inspired.

You can find easy recipes online to help you make your sloe gin, and then enjoy sipping it in the dark evenings in the months ahead – or, if you don't drink gin, you can gift it to friends who do!

WICCAN MYTH CYCLE

The Sun God still roams in the shadows of the woods disguised as the Horned God, but he knows it is nearly time to cast aside his woodland guise and descend to the underworld, where his earthly sacrifice is made. Here, he will await his return to the upper world, which will come when he is reborn at the winter solstice. Meanwhile, the Earth Goddess grows in wisdom and power in her aspects of Crone and the Mother of all the Gods, ready to give birth to him again.

FULL MOON: HUNTER'S/BLOOD MOON

The full moon in October was often referred to as a Hunter's Moon, because when the fields were fallow following a busy harvest, it was easier to spot and chase prey.

The October full moon is also known as the Blood Moon or Sanguine Moon, which may refer to the cull of livestock at the end of the month, or the colour of the moon at its apogee (its closest point to the earth). You may have noticed that at this time of year, the moon may appear in shades of dark orange and deep red.

OCTOBER FULL MOON RITUAL FOR TRANQUILLITY

Drawing down the power of the October full moon will bring you tranquillity and peace in the weeks to come. This is because the full moon in October can occur either in the sign of Libra or Scorpio. The lunar energy of Libra encourages harmony and peace, while Scorpio energy brings quiet confidence and privacy. So whichever sign the full moon falls in this month, these qualities will inspirit a sense of inner calm.

OCT

You will need:
a bowl filled with spring water

1. On the evening of the full moon, place your bowl of spring water outside. Sit or kneel beside the bowl, and gently and slowly swirl one finger in the water in a clockwise direction.

2. Do this three times to invoke the Triple Goddess and her lunar powers, repeating the following as you do so:

For the first circle of the water, say 'Thank you, Triple Goddess, as I hunt for peace.'
For the second circle, say, 'Thank you, Triple Goddess for bringing me serenity.'
For the last circle, say, 'Thank you, Triple Goddess for the joy of autumn and winter.'

3. Leave the bowl of water outside overnight to draw down the energy of the moon and encourage the Triple Goddess to imbue you with serenity.

CONNECT TO NATURE

As the sun moves into secretive Scorpio on around 22 October, you may start to notice an air of mystery abounds. You might come across curious fungi, such as the dangerous-looking but edible scarlet waxcap, or the highly toxic toadstool of fairy tale and literary fame, the fly agaric. (A note: unless you are very confident with identifying varieties of fungi, do not touch any that you see.)

Although the days are growing shorter, more light filters through the trees as leaves begin to fall. We may glimpse shadowy figures, fairies or nature spirits, and when dusk falls, it seems as if something else shifts restlessly in the undergrowth – perhaps the Horned God himself? This mystical time of year reminds us that the landscape is suffused with the supernatural.

In the UK, you can find landscape zodiacs (they also exist in other countries), which are sacred constellation maps plotted out on the surface of the Earth rather than in the sky. They correspond to lanes, hedgerows, field boundaries, streams and so on, and map out the constellational figures of the zodiac. If you ever wish to walk or investigate one of these maps (some well-known ones can be found near Glastonbury, Nuthampstead and Pendle), it will offer you a whole new awareness of our mystical landscape. You may well discover that ley lines, sacred sites, megaliths, sarsen stones (large slabs of sandstone rock, such as those found at Stonehenge), pudding stones (a conglomerate rock composed of rounded pebbles and stones embedded in sand, silt or clay), and other ancient monuments are mysteriously aligned to the zodiac matrix. By visiting these locations, you are engaging in a mystical experience.

FINDING YOUR OWN MYSTICAL LANDSCAPE

Wiccan practice is about immersing yourself in all aspects of nature, not only to connect with the enchantment to be found, but to feel an affinity with the divine. Perhaps Scorpio's secretive energy makes this the perfect time to discover a mystical and sacred landscape of your own?

Go for a walk in a local green space. Look out for large stones, boulders or unusual mounds (moss or weeds may cover a rock completely). Remember, whether they are megaliths, menhirs or something else entirely, all stones are sacred, because they are intrinsic to nature and Mother Earth.

When you find a rock or stone with which you feel an affinity, sit beside it or on it, and express your gratitude to the stone. Although you may not notice anything unusual, if you stay there long enough, you may well feel a mysterious energy emanate around you.

Enjoy being reunited with the supernatural nature of the landscape.

STARLORE

If you look up at the eastern sky, you may spot Andromeda, the closest spiral galaxy to the Milky Way. Made up of nearly a trillion stars, it can be seen on a very clear, dark night as a faint, misty patch just above the Great Square of Pegasus. In the first week of October, usually early in the evening, you can spot the Draconids, a meteor shower that originates from the constellation Draco (the dragon or serpent). This should appear directly overhead, not far from Polaris, the North Star. The second shower of the month occurs usually on around 20 October. This shower is known as the Orionids, and is produced by debris from Halley's comet. It seems to appear from within the constellation Orion. As Orion isn't usually visible until about 11pm at this time of year, you won't see the Orionids peak until after midnight.

THE MYTH OF ANDROMEDA

Andromeda was the beautiful daughter of Aethiopian King Cephus and Queen Cassiopeia. Foolishly, Cassiopeia boasted that her daughter was more radiant than even the sea nymphs, the Nereids. This infuriated Poseidon, who sent a flood and a sea monster to terrorise all. However, an oracle prophesied that if Andromeda was sacrificed to the sea monster, then everyone in Aethiopia would be free once again. Andromeda was chained to a rock and proffered to the sea monster, but the hero Perseus, who was flying over Aethiopia with the aid of a pair of winged sandals, saw Andromeda and fell in love with her at first sight. He was determined to save her from her terrible fate, and, armed with the head of Medusa, his magic sandals and an invisible helmet, Perseus was able to vanquish the monster and free Andromeda. Perseus and Andromeda were then married, and Andromeda became the mother of the royal Perseid line.

If you see Andromeda in the sky, remember that however chained you feel you are to your own personal rock (whether you are bound by your fears, by commitment or by apparent necessity), it is always possible to break free.

TAROT: THE EMPRESS

Traditionally, the card most closely associated with the zodiac sign of Scorpio, which begins on around 20 October, is Death, but I feel it sits better later in the Scorpio period, in the first few weeks in November, after Samhain. To my mind, the card that is best aligned to the idea of harvest and the autumnal energy of October is the card of the Earth Goddess herself, the Empress. As a powerful embodiment of the feminine archetype, the Empress represents creativity, abundance, being at one with nature, and mothering. Whenever you draw this card, you know that it is time to mother your own creativity, and reap the rewards of your own fertile ideas. Meditate on the Empress during the harvest season, for she invokes not only the Earth Goddess but also the spirit of gratitude, blessing and accolade.

NOVEMBER

'Perhaps even these things, one day, will be pleasing to remember.'

VIRGIL,
The Aeneid

NOVEMBER AT A GLANCE

THEMES	impermanence, going with the flow, shadow and light
FESTIVAL/FOCUS	last day of Samhain (1 November)
DEITY	the Crone
CRYSTALS	onyx/turquoise
ELEMENTS	water/fire
FULL MOON	the Dark Moon
TREE	yew
BIRD	rook
PLANT	ivy
ZODIAC	Scorpio/Sagittarius
TAROT	Death

SEASON AND CYCLE

By early November, beech woods are illuminated in golden glory, and shimmering birch leaves dance against the dark green of oaks and the deep red of maples. Squirrels hurriedly scurry for provisions before the encroaching winter (although increasingly you will find that squirrels can be spotted all year round – especially in urban spaces).

On chilly, still mornings, a grey mist hangs ominously in the air above gangs of rooks, who use their beaks to spike the fallow fields and hunt out tasty leatherjackets. Not all is silent, though. November is the season for mating foxes, and you may hear their cries at night, as well as the calls of recently coupled-up tawny owls as they begin to defend their territory through the long winter until they can breed. A sudden influx of blackbirds, who have migrated from colder climates, may begin to appear in gardens, upsetting the local bird population as they flap about, claiming territory. Late November seems to have a neutral energy, with much of nature seemingly in suspended animation.

The lack of light is evident by the end of the month, but we are cheered by the thought that in a few weeks' time, the light will be restored as we welcome the Sun God's return at the winter solstice.

CELEBRATING NOVEMBER

FESTIVAL: SAMHAIN

The Samhain festival of 31 October (see page 166 for more) often lasted into the first few days of November. This was because when bonfires were lit on Samhain Eve, it could often take a day or so for the fires to completely burn out, and while a flame or lingering smoke continued to rise in the air, it was believed the ancestors were still among us. Therefore, it was important to continue to propitiate these souls until the fire was completely extinguished. This period of reflection on the past, the harvest, ancestors, light and fire was a dramatic turning point in the Celtic calendar, so as we come to the end of Samhain, it's appropriate to give a simple thanksgiving for the new Celtic year that is beginning.

LIGHT AND FIRE RITUAL

You will need:
a few handfuls of fallen leaves
a stick
a red crystal (such as red carnelian, red jasper or garnet)

1. On 1 November, go outside and scatter the leaves in a circle around you. Moving in a clockwise direction, turn within the circle and, with your stick, trace a line through the leaves as you affirm: 'From north to east, to south to west, this circle lights the time to rest.'

2. Now place the crystal on the ground beside you to represent 'fire' and 'light'. As you do so, say: 'I will take the light of fire with me through the winter to show me the way, for at the end of Samhain, I am now blessed with my own inner flame to light the path.'

3. Step outside of the circle and walk around once in a clockwise direction, with your stick pointing inwards to the crystal. As you do so, give thanks to the Earth Goddess and Sun God for the changing seasons.

4. Take the crystal in your hand and keep it in a safe place in your home throughout the winter to ignite your own inner warmth, and to inspire and energise you in the months to come.

AFFIRMATIONS FOR THE CHANGING YEAR

With any new year, we set resolutions and find positivity through our thoughts and actions. At Samhain, we have left the old Celtic year behind and now face a new one. Traditionally, witches wrote down not only spells and rituals in their Book of Shadows, but also positive statements, as if to cast a 'spell' of self-empowerment around them for the months to come.

So to find light among the darker days, and enjoy the experience of positivity throughout November, write down or repeat the following affirmations, as and when you feel the moment is right:

'The end is my beginning.'

'The present is the past of my future, so I live in the moment that is all three.'

'I am at one with nature, and everything fills me with delight, even the end of summer, for I am winter too.'

'My journey goes deep into myself, and with every step I take, I discover what I can relinquish and what I can develop.'

'Autumn may take us away from summer, but it leads us to the mystery of winter and beyond.'

'What would I most like to offer to the world? Considering this question will lead me on to the right path.'

'When I come from a place of inner tranquillity, I find peace all around.'

'Every ending lays the foundation for something new to begin.'

'I embrace change and follow the seasons gladly, as the summer follows spring, as the autumn follows summer, as the winter follows autumn, as the spring follows winter.'

'I give gratitude to the changing seasons, and at every moment I see the beauty within nature.'

'I look in the mirror of the winter of myself, to find the depths of spring and summer reflected there.'

'Thanks to the Sun God for his light that has been and is yet to come; thanks to the Earth Goddess for the bounty we have had, and that we will have again.'

If you will be spending more of your days indoors as winter approaches, turn to your Book of Shadows again and write a poem, a piece of prose, or a letter to yourself expressing your sense of 'endings and beginnings'. If you don't feel inspired to write, the next best thing is to find a 'poem', quote or any phrase or piece of writing with a theme that resonates with your 'end of summer, beginning of winter feeling', then copy it into your book.

You will need:
a white tealight candle (to represent beginnings)
a black tealight candle (to represent endings)
your Book of Shadows
a pen

1. Light the candles and sit down with your Book of Shadows.
2. Take up your pen and enjoy a moment for creative writing, or writing out the poem or text you have found.
3. When you have finished, focus on the flames of the candles, then read aloud what you have written to affirm your trust in and acceptance of this transitional period.
4. Blow out the black candle first, and affirm that you have written about an ending, and then blow out the white candle and affirm that you have penned your 'beginning'. Then follow through with your intentions for the rest of winter.

THE NORTH WIND SPELL

Son of the Greek goddess of the dawn, Eos, Boreas was the god of the north wind, storms and winter. He was one of the four gods known as the Anemoi, who personified the winds of the four cardinal directions. Boreas comes to us increasingly frequently in November, often lashing us with howling winds, freezing rain and unwelcome weather. Yet if we change our perspective and metaphorically invite the wind, the cold and the rain with open arms, we can find joy in the changing weather and go with the flow of its energy, rather than resisting it. So why not try this simple spell to ensure the wind blows in fresh ideas and a joyful outlook for the weeks to come?

You will need:
a piece of paper and a pen
4 white tealight candles
1 blue crystal (colour of the west)
1 red crystal (colour of the south)
1 yellow crystal (colour of the east)
1 green crystal (colour of the north)

1. On your piece of paper, draw a cross to mark the four points of the compass. Write 'N' at the top, 'E' on the right, 'S' at the bottom, and 'W' on the left.
2. Place one tealight at each point of the compass, and light them carefully.
3. Hold the four stones in your hand and say: 'Boreas, spirit of the north wind, I thank you for blowing

fresh ideas to me in the coming weeks, and for bringing me the joy of winter; so I align with nature's ways, whether north, south, east or west. Blessed be.'

4. Hold all the stones to your belly for a moment to charge their energy to you. When you are ready, place the green stone to the north, the red stone to the south, the yellow stone to the east, and the blue stone to the west.

5. Now blow out the tealight candles to seal your petition to the north wind to send you beneficial energy and a sense of being at one with the winter. Leave the stones in place overnight to encourage new ideas to blow into your life and for planning a successful future.

MYTH

The Crone has long been a symbol of old age, winter, the waning and dark of the moon phase, destruction and death. As the Dark Goddess, she appears in many guises, such as Hecate, Hel, Ceridwen, Kali the Destroyer, Macha, Morgan, and the third aspect of the Triple Goddess, the Crone. In Wicca, she is the wise woman, the Celtic Cailleach, and a symbol of endings and beginnings. The early depiction of the Crone as a wiser, older woman may in fact have its origins in the Greek goddess Rhea, who was both the older sibling and the wife of Cronus (Saturn in Roman myth), and was known as Mother of the Gods. It was prophesied that Cronus would, in time, be overthrown by one of his own children, mirroring how he had usurped his own father's position as king of the gods. Fuelled by fear, he devoured each of his children as soon as they were born. Rhea, unwilling to lose another child to her husband, decided to take matters into her own hands. When her sixth child, Zeus, was born, she switched him with a stone wrapped in swaddling clothes and presented this stone to Cronus instead, hiding away the real Zeus in a cave on Mount Ida. When Zeus came of age, he realised Cronus's greatest fear by returning to Mount Olympus with the help of his mother and forcing his father to disgorge his siblings, who became the gods of Olympia.

When we think of Rhea as the Crone, we realise that the Crone does not just symbolise the end of life. She is also the creator, who protects wisely, midwifing the cycle of death and birth, and the taking but also the giving of life.

RITUAL FOR CALLING UPON THE CRONE

Throughout the year, we can call upon the Crone for her wisdom. But as she comes to prominence in the winter months, this is an auspicious time to call on her, either to help us overcome a fear, a loss or a change of circumstance, or to help us explore deeper truths about who we are and where we are going.

You will need:
a blue tealight candle
a seasonal plant or leaf

1. Safely light the blue candle to represent the glowing light of the winter months, and place an offering of a seasonal plant or leaf before the candle.

2. As you do so, say: 'Greetings to you, the Goddess of Winter, for your protection and support. As the Wheel turns, so I turn to you for your wisdom. Bless my ancestors and all who live in this present moment, and future ones, too, for as the Wheel turns, I turn with you. Send me your wise words so the deepest truth will be mine to uncover.'

3. Focus on the candle for a few minutes, and breathe in the spirit of the winter and the Crone, whose wisdom will come to you as insight and self-awareness through the winter days.

WICCAN MYTH CYCLE

The Sun God has descended to the underworld, his fading light now a dim reminder of his glorious summer past, yet also a sign that his resurrection is nigh. The Horned God of the dark forest (an aspect of the Sun God) has been cast out by the Earth Goddess, for now she holds the power of winter as the Crone, the wise woman, and the Queen of Winter who rules the dark days between Samhain and Beltane. She knows that very soon, she will give birth to the Sun God, who will be her son and later her lover.

FULL MOON: THE DARK MOON

The November full moon is often known as the Dark Moon. In fact, this moon is similar in energy to the waning moon phase of the lunar cycle. The waning phase is a time when we can dig deep into understanding our true intentions, looking back at what we've achieved and considering the choices we have made. It is an opportunity to review and rest before the next lunar phase. Similarly, November's Dark Moon encourages us to consider the intentions that we set earlier in the year and reflect on any gains we feel we have made. The focus is not on achievement, but on recognising that it is possible to make progress even if we aren't yet exactly where we want to be.

DARK MOON RITUAL

Try out this ritual to help you reflect on, revise and review your intentions.

You will need:
a piece of black tourmaline, obsidian or onyx
a piece of clear quartz

1. On the evening of the full moon, place your crystals side by side on your altar or table.
2. Pick up the black crystal and hold it gently to your forehead. Imagine the darkness of winter, the dark of the moon and the blackness of the long nights. Now, just for a moment, let the crystal fill you with

darkness, but always with awareness of its beauty, and its part to play in the cycle of life, death and rebirth.

3. Next, pick up the clear quartz crystal and hold it gently to your forehead. Close your eyes for a moment and imagine the light returning to the world. You may even feel the energy of the crystal imbuing you with bright power.

4. As the full moon reflects the light of the sun, November reflects the summer that's gone and the summer towards which you are moving. If you open your eyes and gaze into the crystal, you may glimpse the sunlight and the summer, for it is always there.

5. Place your crystals back on your altar or table when you feel intuitively that the moment is right. You are now ready to review, revive and rework your intentions if need be, in preparation for the changing energy of this season.

CONNECT TO NATURE

Nature is inert right now, with the majestic oak trees usually the last of the deciduous trees to lose their leaves as we move towards midwinter. Silver birch trees stand out in the grey landscape with their brilliant silvery-white trunks. Their boughs bend in the cruellest of winds, and shake off early snowfall with the ease of a dog shaking water off its back. Yet, there are some trees, such as the yew, which lurk ominously in the dullness of the days, and have long been associated with death.

Yew trees are commonly found in Britain, but are often avoided due to superstitions, their menacing black trunks and toxic attributes (they are extremely poisonous). In *Macbeth*, Shakespeare had his title character concoct a poisonous brew made of 'slips of yew, silvered in the moon's eclipse'.

Despite these sinister connotations, the yew was sacred to the Druids and in early Celtic traditions was thought to represent longevity, regeneration and resurrection. This is because yew trees can re-root from their old drooping boughs when they touch the ground. This ancient association with revival was assimilated into Christianity and linked to the story of the resurrection of Jesus. Yews are commonly found in British churchyards for that reason, but as many churches were built on earlier pagan sacred sites, the more ancient trees are likely to already have been in situ long before the churches were built.

So this November, why not show your respect for these very ancient sacred trees? All you need to do is visit an old churchyard to find one, then just look at it for a while, admiring it and remembering the lesson it has for us: that if we spread our metaphorical boughs wide and low, open up and try to be more humble and accepting of ourselves, we will find the strength to revive and bring to life our deepest truth.

One of the best-known constellations of winter, Orion, now returns to the south of the night sky, and we will see more and more of this superb constellation throughout the colder months. Two of Orion's stars, Betelgeuse and Rigel, are known to be among the ten brightest stars in the sky.

Around mid-November, look out for the Leonid meteor shower. If you stand facing north-east, then turn slightly to the right, you will find Leo, from which the shower's radiance originates. November is also one of the best months to view the Pleiades, or Seven Sisters asterism, just above the constellation Taurus. In Greek mythology, the seven sisters were the daughters of the Titan Atlas, who, after the Titans were defeated by the Olympian gods, was condemned by Zeus to carry the heavens on his shoulders for eternity. The hunter Orion took advantage of Atlas's burden and chased his seven daughters with the intention of raping them. Zeus intervened, however, and transformed the sisters first into doves, and then into stars to protect them from Orion and to placate their father. Orion is said to still try to pursue them across the night sky, but he can never catch them.

NOV

THE LOST PLEIAD

Known as the 'Lost Pleiad', one of the stars in the asterism is so faint that it can hardly be seen. Curiously, the more you try to focus on it, the more it seems to fade away in the sky. This perhaps resonates with one myth about the Pleiades, which describes how the youngest sister, Merope, married the tyrannical King Sisyphus and became a mortal. It was dictated that her fate would be to gradually fade away, while another myth says that she hides her face in shame because of her love for the mortal, despotic king.

TAROT: DEATH

As Samhain is symbolic of endings and beginnings, so too is the Death card. Although often feared in a Tarot reading, the Death card has a positive meaning. In fact, we should welcome this card, as it tells us to embrace change rather than fear it. It is an archetypal energy, concerning transition, movement and the benefit of transformation. It tells you that something is ending, and something else is beginning; the end of a cycle has come, and the old cycle will now give way to an exciting new one. Reflect on the Death card during November, for it brings with it the chance for positive changes in the months to come.

DECEMBER

'In the bleak midwinter, frosty wind made moan,
Earth stood hard as iron, water like a stone.'

CHRISTINA ROSSETTI,
'In the Bleak Midwinter'

DECEMBER AT A GLANCE

THEMES	renaissance, celebration, reawakening
FESTIVAL/FOCUS	winter solstice
DEITY	the Sun God
CRYSTALS	turquoise/malachite
ELEMENTS	fire/earth
FULL MOON	Oak Moon
TREE	holly
BIRD	robin
PLANT	mistletoe
ZODIAC	Sagittarius/Capricorn
TAROT	Temperance

SEASON AND CYCLE

December derives from the Latin *decem*, meaning 'ten', as it was the tenth month in the pre-Julian Roman calendar. In the northern hemisphere, December weather can range from cold and dark to foggy and grey, or from torrential rain to crisp, bright sunlight (if only for a few hours). As Mother Nature takes a winter respite, the darkest days of the year are upon us. Although the darkness may seem overwhelming, the winter solstice marks a turning point after which the days will gradually grow longer, and with this, the mood at the end of December is more forgiving and encourages us to look to the future. The change may be hard to detect at first, but just knowing that we are once again priming ourselves for spring and rebirth heralds an uplifting, spirited energy.

The joy to be found in December is in our ability to celebrate the darkness by shining our own light, whether via the glitter of Yule, solstice and other festivities, or via our inner flame. We can now give gratitude to what has been, and give offerings to what will be.

THE ROBIN

An icon of the winter season, this perky little bird has, for centuries, been a symbolic messenger of rebirth, good luck and happiness in myth, poetry and art. The old adage, 'When robins appear, loved ones are near,' refers to the belief that robins can bring us messages of hope and comfort from loved ones who have passed over. Some say the robin gets its red breast from the blood of Christ, while others suggest that the bird was scorched when it flew too close to the Sun God. Perhaps the robin's chirpy, friendly nature tells us that even in the harshest of winters, the warmth of spring will soon be with us.

CELEBRATING DECEMBER

FESTIVAL: WINTER SOLSTICE

Many Wiccans consider the birth of the Sun God as the start of a new solar cycle. Of course, the Wheel never stops turning, so you are free to mark the solstice, Samhain or any of the other sabbats as the ending and beginning of the seasonal year. It is really down to personal preference.

When the sun arrives at zero degrees Capricorn, it is now at its nadir (lowest point), marking the shortest day in the northern hemisphere. Over the next six months, the sun will climb gradually towards its zenith (highest point), when we reach the summer solstice. Right now, though, there is a sense of stillness in nature, which is likely to be in direct contrast to the hustle and bustle that many of us experience during the festive season. The winter solstice also aligns with the traditional Germanic observation of Yule, and many Wiccans use the two terms synonymously for this season of the Wheel of the Year.

Yule was a festive period for folk to decorate trees and burn logs in the home fire to bring good luck for the coming year. Although the exact date of observation is debated among scholars, and could fall any time from late December through to the end of January, Yule was first identified with the worship of Odin in Norse mythology, and the mythical Wild Hunt held in the darkest nights of winter.

The Wild Hunt is a shared motif in many Norse and Celtic mythologies. The hunt was usually led by a mythological character who was escorted by ghosts or supernatural beings on the chase for lost souls. One example is the Welsh huntsman Gwyn ap Nudd, who rode a demon horse accompanied by the dogs of hell. The dark nights of winter represented the underworld and death, which created fear among most folk that the sun would never return, leaving them in permanent darkness and at the mercy of the 'supernatural hunt'. So Yule was a time for both propitiating the supernatural world, but also appealing to the Sun God to return. Yule was also identified with Modraniht (Mother's Night), the Anglo-Saxon celebration of 24 December, and in the ninth century, the word became associated with the traditional Christian celebration of the birth of Jesus.

Whatever personal belief or tradition you and your family choose to follow, this is the season to make merry, to bring light into the darkness and to lighten other people's lives with kindness, gentleness and compassion. This is a time to gather together, to feast and laugh, to enjoy the camaraderie of friends and to reach out to loved ones far away. Create some warmth around you and thank the sun for its life-giving cycle.

NEOLITHIC WINTER SOLSTICE

The ancient Neolithic passage tomb at Newgrange, Ireland, dating to around 3200 BCE, is aligned to the sunrise at the winter solstice. When the sun reaches a certain angle at the moment of the solstice, its rays shine through an opening known as the 'roof-box', then travel along the nineteen-metre passage. As the sun continues to rise, more and more light illuminates the passage, representing the sun's triumph over darkness. For ancient peoples, this must have been a moment of great reverence. This sacred place affirmed that the sun would return to illuminate their lives and ensure the fertility of crops for another year.

A traditional Wiccan celebration for the winter solstice is to honour the return of the light and the birth of the Sun God, preferably on the solstice day itself. This ritual honours the changing influence from the 'old dark of winter' to the 'new light of winter' by calling on the four elements and the deities to encourage harmony and positive new beginnings

You will need:
a green tealight candle (for the Earth Goddess)
a red tealight candle (for the Sun God)
2 white tealight candles (one to represent fire, and another to bring the ceremony to a close)
a crystal of your choice (to represent earth)
a feather or fallen leaf (to represent air)
a shell or cup of water (to represent water)

1. First, give thanks for the never-ending synergy between the Earth Goddess and the Sun God by lighting their respective candles.

2. As you light the green candle, say, 'I give thanks to the Earth Goddess in all her emanations, as Maiden, Mother and Crone, and for the rebirth of the Sun God at this time, who will shine new light upon us all. Blessed be.'

3. As you light the Sun God's candle, say, 'I give thanks to the Sun God, who awakens from the dark of winter and is reborn, ready to light our way again.'

DEC

4. Now place the attributes of the four elements in a line before you, from left to right, starting with fire, then earth, then air and then water. Finally, say, 'I give gratitude to the four elements of fire, earth, air and water for this solstice time when the solar light returns to bring joy to the Earth.'

5. Some Wiccans may light a bonfire (an ancient ritual to welcome the power of the sun) or a hearth fire, but for safety, you only need to light the white candle as a sign of your respect and belief in the Sun God as he now begins his ascent towards the summer solstice. When you are ready to leave your ritual, safely snuff out the candles and give thanks: 'Blessed be the Sun God and Earth Goddess for this moment of joy.'

A RITUAL FOR REFLECTION AND GRATITUDE

On the day of the solstice, you may like to sit and reflect for a while on what this day might mean for you personally. It may be a time to express gratitude.

You will need:
3 white tealight candles
3 red tealight candles

1. Place your white and red tealight candles carefully on your altar. Light each one, and then focus for a moment on the flames.

2. Give thanks to yourself and to the people around you. The spirit of the solstice is one of appreciation, renewal, gratitude and love, so appreciate your own gifts and virtues, not just those of others. Safely snuff out the candles once you're ready.

3. At sunset, take a walk outside and look up at the setting sun. Remember that although it is the shortest day of the year, from now on there will be more light, as the Sun God's power returns to brighten our world.

SATURNALIA

Around the time of the winter solstice, an ancient Roman festival known as Saturnalia was celebrated to honour the god Saturn. Saturn was thought to have once ruled the mythical 'Golden Age', an era of wealth, success, joviality and, above all, pleasure. Saturnalia was a festival of light leading up to the winter solstice and beyond, and over a period of a few days to a week, everyone was given free rein to indulge in all forms of earthly delight. To the Romans, the actual winter solstice (in the old Roman calendar, this fell on 25 December) was also celebrated, heralding the return of *sol invictus*, or 'the invincible sun'.

To celebrate the return of the invincible Sun God, perform a simple standing-still ritual, like the one you did at the summer solstice (see page 96).

You will need:
3 red tealight candles
3 white tealight candles

1. Place the three candles on your altar and light each one. Stand still in front of the candles for a minute.
2. Next, show your appreciation for the Sun God by raising your arms above your head as a salutation. Bow forward and touch the ground (if you physically can't do this, then try it from a sitting position) to show your appreciation that the sun gives life to the earth, and the earth now returns the Sun God to us, to lighten up our world.
3. Return to your standing position and affirm the following: 'This midwinter is as beautiful as the summer, autumn, and spring. Thank you, Sun God, for keeping me vitalised, and for showing me how each cycle is a treasured reminder of life on this earth.'

MISTLETOE

To the Druids, mistletoe represents the sacred and mystical gateway between sky and earth, and could only be cut down with a golden scythe to ensure it remained magical. The gold symbolised the sun, and the scythe itself, the moon. One Norse myth recounts how the youthful god Balder, who was the son of the sorceress Frigg and the chief of gods Odin, was prophesied to die young. Frigg told the trickster god Loki that every creature and plant on earth had sworn never to harm her son, except mistletoe, saying: 'East of Valhalla grows a plant called mistletoe; it seemed to me too young to swear.' Loki, who was always in disputes with Balder, made a mistletoe arrow or spear and shot it at Balder, killing him. Frigg was distraught and her tears turned to white berries, covering the plant as a symbol of her love for him. In memory of her son, Frigg vowed to place a kiss on all those who passed beneath the mistletoe. This ancient myth may be the origin of the 'kissing beneath the mistletoe ritual' practised during the festive period.

MYTH

The Sun God, in most mythologies, is usually identified with the divine masculine principle. Although sun goddesses also appear in world mythology, for the purpose of this book, we'll stick with the one sun god who outshines all the others: Helios.

Helios, the Greek sun god, was the brother of Selene, the moon, and Eos, the dawn. Helios was later rivalled by Apollo, the god of light, who was identified as the supreme solar deity. However, Helios remained the personification of the sun itself, fathering many children, such as the sorceress Circe, who was the product of his affair with the ocean nymph, Perse.Rather like the Egyptian solar deity Ra, Helios is a god who both sees and hears everything, and who can spy on gods and mortals alike. Many myths are attributed to Helios, who was called on in magic spells, petitioned to witness promises and oaths, and invoked as a diviner of dreams.

A RITUAL TO CONNECT TO HELIOS

Use this ritual to experience and connect to Helios's energy, and to help you take practical action.

You will need:
a piece of paper and a pen

1. Make a promise to yourself to do something practical: anything to which you can commit yourself in the near future.

2. Write down your promise on a piece of paper, and then take the piece of paper outside with you. Hold it up to the sky, and say: 'Helios, I promise that I will fulfil this commitment to act before the [a date of your choosing]. You, the sun, bear witness to my oath, for I will not betray this promise.'

3. Dispose of the paper, and trust that Helios will lend you his light to encourage you to deliver your promise.

WICCAN MYTH CYCLE

The Sun God's power has diminished to such an extent that only a faint light remains in the winter skies. At his demise, we experience the shortest day. His journey is at its end, and as he languishes in the underworld, the Earth Goddess begins to feel the stirrings of new life within. She is preparing to give birth to the solar deity; once this is done, she will move from being the Mother to the Crone of winter. As the day of the solstice arrives, so too does the Sun God's rebirth, and with it his promise of another year of light and love.

FULL MOON: OAK MOON

Some mythological sources suggest that the name Oak Moon derives from the traditional Druid ritual of harvesting mistletoe from oak trees during and just after the winter solstice full moon. The plant was believed to protect against evil, and to boost fertility and vitality. However, according to botanical experts, it is actually quite rare to find mistletoe growing in oak trees (in the UK, at any rate), as it more commonly grows in poplar, willow and apple. However, the name of the Oak Moon could also allude to the strength and endurance of the oak tree, and how we all need an extra shot of courage and determination to get through the winter.

OAK TREE RITUAL

Oak trees are associated with strength and determination. Wiccans visit these trees in winter to connect with their magic powers, and also to give thanks to the dryads – the oak tree nymphs – for protecting the trees.

1. First, touch the trunk and the bark of an oak tree. The north-facing side may be covered in moss or lichen, while the south-facing side might be dry and rough, perhaps with bark bleached smooth by the hotter sun of summer.

2. Hold your palm flat to the trunk and imagine drawing in its power. Imagine that you are being filled with empowering energy, right from its deepest roots to the highest point of its branches. Imagine you are connected to the magic of the tree, and as you stand for a few minutes in awe at its majesty, you will begin to experience that spiritual connection too.

3. End by giving thanks to the dryads for protecting the oak, and to the oak for its generous power, and then give blessings to all of nature.

CONNECT TO NATURE

Why not immerse yourself in the winter landscape by going out to observe whatever you can to give you a different perspective on the natural world? Observe how different the trees look now; see the way that they are more defined by their overall shape or structure, not just by their canopy of leaves.

If you walk along a seashore, the grey, wintry ocean may suddenly turn blue as the clouds part and the sky opens up; as you walk in the countryside, the frost thaws, the ice-covered puddles crack under your feet, and the wind suddenly whirls around you. This has its own beauty, its own magic, and, as such, the essence of winter is as empowering as that of summer. This means seeing the seasons of summer and winter not as opposites, one better than the other, but as one and the same. Albert Camus wrote, 'In the depths of winter, I finally learned that within me there lay an invincible summer.' Perhaps, as Wiccans, we can see that within us there lies an invincible winter, too.

The changing landscape reminds you that this part of the cycle of nature is also part of you. You are changing with every season, growing, evolving and discovering your true potential, so experience all the seasons for what they are, neither one better than the other, and all 'invincible'.

CANDLES AND EVERGREEN GODDESS SPELL

A traditional Wiccan ritual at winter solstice was to place candles on an outdoor evergreen tree (a symbol of ancient wisdom) to honour the Earth Goddess and cast a spell for her continuing kindness to allow all of nature to blossom again. However, lighting candles outside is not to be recommended, as the wind may blow them over or blow the flame into the tree. So here's an alternative way to perform this ritual.

You will need:
a large evergreen branch or bough
4 red tealight candles (to represent the two solstices and two equinoxes)
4 green tealight candles (to represent the four cross-quarter days)
a piece of black tourmaline or onyx, or just a very black stone (for the Earth Goddess/Crone of winter)

1. Place the bough on your altar or table, then arrange the eight tealights around it as the points of the Wheel of the Year. The north is associated with the winter solstice, so begin there with a red candle, then arrange the remaining candles around the Wheel aligning with the solstices, equinoxes and cross-quarter days. Ensure that the candles are well distanced from the foliage.

2. When you have marked out your Wheel, place the stone in the middle of the evergreen bough. Finally, light the candles.

3. Call in the Earth Goddess by pointing a finger at the crystal in the centre and saying: 'I call on you, Crone of winter, Earth Goddess of all of nature. Sanctify this evergreen altar with growing power so that throughout the year, we all can blossom and grow and return full cycle to this moment again. So mote it be.' (If you prefer, you can make up your own wording here.)

4. For a few moments, or for as long as you feel is right, focus on each flame of each candle, starting with east and moving in a sun-wise direction (so going to south, then west, then north, then back to east).

5. When you are ready, snuff each candle in turn, and when all is still, take the crystal from the centre and hold it close to your belly. Say: 'Thank you, Earth Goddess, Crone of winter, for imbuing all of nature with your goodness for another turn of the Wheel.'

6. Replace the crystal in the centre of the evergreen bough until the end of the solstice day, or for the rest of the festive season, then keep the crystal in a safe place until the following winter solstice.

STARLORE

One constellation high in the northern sky at this time of year is the sign of Gemini, or the twins Castor and Pollux (who were, in fact, half-brothers). Their mother was the

Spartan queen Leda. Castor's father was the Spartan king, while Pollux's father was Zeus. Pollux asked Zeus to let him share his immortality with Castor, so to keep them together, Zeus transformed them into the constellation Gemini. Throughout December and January, you can find Gemini by locating Orion, then drawing an imaginary line northeast through Rigel and Betelgeuse to lead you to the stars Castor and Pollux. Mid-December also marks the peak of the Geminid meteor shower, when shooting stars illuminate the darkness on a clear night. Although they can appear in any part of the sky, they originate from Gemini.

As you gaze at the constellation, reflect on the nature of the twins, and how Pollux shared his immortality with his brother. We are of the earth and also of the stars; we are flesh and bones, but we are imbued with soul, and the divine flows through us. Pollux shared his immortality with Castor, and likewise we need to learn to share our love and compassion with others.

TAROT: TEMPERANCE

At the solstice, the energy changes from the fire sign of Sagittarius to the earth sign of Capricorn. We are taken on a journey to help us realise that all our personal reflections of the past weeks are now about to be activated. However, Capricorn is a sign of caution and tempering our impulses. So this card is concerned with moderation, compromise and self-control. In fact, by 'tempering' our desires, we may bring harmony to our lives and realise that balance and the acceptance of our faults, and those of others, will encourage success in all we do as we move towards the next turn of the Wheel.

JANUARY

'I wonder if the snow loves the trees and fields, that it kisses them so gently? And then it covers them up snug, you know, with a white quilt; and perhaps it says, "Go to sleep, darlings, till the summer comes again."'

LEWIS CARROLL,
Through the Looking Glass

JANUARY AT A GLANCE

THEMES	rest, contemplation, recuperation
FESTIVAL/FOCUS	none
DEITY	the Cailleach
CRYSTALS	garnet/amber
ELEMENTS	earth/air
FULL MOON	Quiet/Wolf Moon
TREE	hazel
BIRD	blue tit
PLANT	hellebore
ZODIAC	Capricorn/Aquarius
TAROT	the Star

SEASON AND CYCLE

In January, it may feel as if we are walking amid the bare bones of winter, but the Earth is tilting slowly back towards the sun, bringing more light to illuminate our lives.

January was named after the Roman deity Janus who could see the future and the past simultaneously. He was depicted with two faces and was the god of thresholds, beginnings and endings, which was why he was chosen to rule the first month of the calendar year.

In relation to the Wheel of the Year, January is a transitional, threshold month. Lodged between the winter solstice and Imbolc, it is a period for rest and recuperation. Mammals tuck themselves away, insects hide in nooks and crannies, and plants conserve energy for the arrival of spring. Gangs of sparrows may still chirp about looking for food, and flocks of tits and finches thrive on our bird feeders. The sight of early spring shoots are a sign of the light to come. Welcome this peaceful time, immerse yourself in its tranquillity, and welcome and feed the birds too.

CELEBRATING JANUARY

WASSAILING

As there are no major Wiccan festivals in January, why not enjoy a traditional Anglo-Saxon fruit tree celebration instead? Wassailing takes place on Twelfth Night (associated with Epiphany, so 5 or 6 January) and is believed to ensure a beneficial fruit harvest later in the year – both in terms of literal fruit, and also in terms of helping your resolutions and plans bear fruit later in the year. The word 'wassail' is thought to be derived from the medieval toast *'was hail'*, meaning 'good health', rooted in the Norse words *ves heil*.

Traditional Anglo-Saxon wassailing was first recorded in the medieval period, and involved a trip to an orchard to toast and give offerings to the tree spirits or gods. The wassail bowl, a large vessel usually made of wood or pewter, was filled with wassail – mulled cider, wine or ale – and was passed around the participants to drink to honour the spirits. In some localised folk customs, bread wafers were floated on the surface as offerings, and by the end of the eighteenth century, the 'toasting' of the apple tree spirits involved hanging pieces of bread soaked in wassail on the boughs or leaving them at the foot of the trees. By the beginning of the twentieth century, literal toast was used to 'toast' the spirits for a beneficial harvest. An incantation was then recited or sung, and the remaining wassail was poured over the roots.

TRADITIONAL WASSAILING RITUAL

Here's a way to do a little wassailing to ensure a good harvest without having to visit an orchard. If you are lucky enough to have a fruit tree in your garden, you can go and commune with the tree spirits that way.

You will need:

an apple tree, or a small branch of an apple or other fruit tree, or an image of one

4 slices of dry toast

2 cups of wassail (mulled cider, ale or wine, or a mulled non-alcoholic drink, if you prefer)

1. Do this outside if you can. Standing by your apple tree or branch, break the toast into large pieces and soak them for just a few seconds in one of your cups of wassail.

2. Place the pieces of toast on the tree/branch or tie them to it.

3. Admire the bough and raise the other cup to the tree spirit for a good crop in the months to come. If you are outdoors with a real tree, pour a little wassail around the roots, too.

4. Thank the tree spirits, and leave your toast votives overnight to encourage a bumper fruit harvest in more ways than one.

In Greek mythology, Hestia was the daughter of Cronus and Rhea, and was a virgin goddess by choice. Hestia ruled not only sacred and public hearths – the most sacred of all being the one at the temple of Apollo at Delphi – but also the home hearth. The centre of the home was the fireplace, and a family's spiritual and emotional health was dependent on honouring Hestia every day when preparing meals, keeping warm or making sacrificial offerings to the gods. She was called on to protect all the family, and people honoured her by maintaining her fire and making offerings of bread and wine.

January is often the time we think about future home improvements or how to improve our family relationships. After the excesses of the festive season, it can feel like a pause before we get on with living life to the full again. So to encourage protective energy for your family and home, call on Hestia and her associated crystal, the garnet, an empowering symbol of love, protection and rekindling one's inner spiritual flame.

You will need:
4 basil leaves (for physical protection)
4 pieces of garnet (for protection against negativity)
a red tealight candle

1. On a table or your altar, form a cross using the four basil leaves, and then place a piece of garnet on each leaf. Put the red tealight candle in the centre,

light it, and focus on the flame for a moment. Turn your gaze to each of the garnets, and as you look at each one, say the appropriate line:

> 'With garnet north, my family's worth
> With garnet east, my home's a feast
> With garnet south, no hand to mouth
> With garnet west, we live our best.'

2. Call on Hestia to bless your garnets and your home, by saying: 'Hestia, welcome to my hearth. I give gratitude to you for the warmth of your fire, for the blessing of these garnets, each a treasured symbol of home, family, peace and harmony.'

3. Blow out the candle when you feel ready and leave the grid overnight to draw Hestia's power into your home. In the morning, remove the garnets and put them in a special place to keep them safe.

4. You and your home will be protected and revitalised throughout the next cycle of the Wheel, when you can repeat this protection ritual once more.

A DIVINATION RITUAL

As we've learned, Janus is the god of thresholds, but he is also the all-seeing god of past, present and future. So while it is his month, try out this simple divination ritual to help you make a choice about something that is important to you right now.

You will need:

3 stones or crystals of your choice (to represent the past, present and future)

1. Take the first stone and say, 'This is the stone of the past.' Turn it round and round in your hand, and then, when you feel the moment is right, cast it on to the ground before you.
2. Now take the second stone and say, 'This is the stone of the present.' Turn and cast it as above.
3. Take the third stone and say, 'This is the stone of the future,' then turn and cast it once more.
4. Now look at where the stones have fallen. If the past stone is nearest to you, then this means you must trust the last gut feeling you had about your issue before you did this ritual. If the present stone is nearest to you, then trust any flash of insight you have right now. And if the future stone is nearest to you, trust any 'sign' that comes to you in the next twenty-four hours.

MYTH

We first met the Gaelic Cailleach in February in the form of the Scottish Beira, Queen of Winter, an ancient deity who ruled the winter months between Samhain (1 November) and Beltane (1 May). There are many legends surrounding her in Celtic mythology. As a Crone archetype, the Cailleach was feared and revered for her power to govern winter and prolong it if she felt so inclined.

In Ireland, she was said to be responsible for the formation of many of the country's most outstanding landmarks. According to legend, she either dropped or threw stones from her apron as she passed through the land, and these grew into rock formations or mountains. A large rock situated at Coulagh Bay in County Cork is believed to be symbolic of her head and face. As she stared out to sea, waiting in vain for her husband, the sea god Manannan mac Lir, to return, her face turned to stone. Visitors to the site often leave coins, stones or other offerings to appease the Cailleach.

THE CAILLEACH RITUAL

1. To petition the Cailleach for a contented winter for you, your family and loved ones, visit a local standing stone, menhir or large rock, as these are the most fitting places to leave a votive for her. If you don't have easy access to one of these spots, you can place a photo of a standing stone with which you feel an affinity on your altar instead.

2. Look out for a stone or pebble in your garden, green space, countryside, or when you reach your chosen location. In Wicca, we often discover that a random stone 'sees' us, 'calls' to us, and we know we must pick it up. This is often a moment to cherish: a moment when we realise that the divine is calling us, as we call on the divine.

3. So, pick up this stone that calls to you and place it on top of or beside your chosen rock. Standing

beside it, trace in the air the sign of the pentagram (to represent the four elements and the quintessential fifth). As you do so, say:

> 'Great Crone of winter, bless us until the dark is replaced by light. We acknowledge your power and bless you for winter's being. Bless this stone as you bless all the rocks of the earth and fill it with your power. I offer this stone as a votive of contentment. Blessed be.'

4. Leave your shrine, knowing that the Cailleach may prolong the winter cold, but she will ensure you are well and happy whatever the weather.

WICCAN MYTH CYCLE

Like most of nature, the Sun God and Earth Goddess are hidden away at this time. The child Sun God, hiding in his sheltered dark winter palace, is becoming aware of his growing power as he slowly revives. The Earth Goddess is also gradually transforming from the Crone of winter into the Maiden of spring. She knows she must wait a little longer until she is purified of her winter guise at Imbolc. Soon after, she will be ready to lead the Sun God on a merry dance in the woods.

FULL MOON: QUIET/WOLF MOON

Although the January full moon is often known as the Wolf Moon, for the purposes of this book, I have chosen to side with the Celtic tradition of the Quiet Moon, as it fits well with this month's theme of silence, tranquillity and reflection, and seems fitting to mark the last chapter of this book.

QUIET MOON RITUAL

During the full moon, perform the following ritual to connect to the lunar energy of quietness, recuperation and revival.

You will need:
a white tealight candle
3 pieces of selenite or moonstone

1. On a table or your altar, light the candle and place the three crystals in front of it.
2. Pick up the crystal on the left and hold it close to your belly as you say, 'This crystal brings me the power of the moonlight in the dark of winter.'
3. Place the left crystal back on the table, then pick up the middle crystal. As you hold it to your belly, say, 'This crystal casts the light of quietness, peace and repose in the dark of winter.'
4. Place the middle crystal back on the table, then pick up the crystal on the right. As you hold it to

your belly, say, 'This crystal reflects my own light and revival in the dark of winter.'

5. Finally, gaze into the candle flame for a few minutes and reflect on your past, present and future. As you do so, say, 'The past is where I have been; it is quiet, but unforgotten. The present is where I recuperate; it is now, but soon to be past. And the future is where I revive; it is soon to be now.'

6. Blow out the candle and leave your crystals in place overnight to charge them with lunar energy. Keep the crystals somewhere safe, and you will feel revived and restored, ready for the year ahead.

CONNECT TO NATURE

Although it may feel like a small gesture, using a bird feeder for the local wild birds is enough to help you feel a connection with nature during this cold and seemingly long month – and perhaps more importantly, they may feel gladdened and connected to you, and thankful for your help. Encourage more birds to flock to your garden, your terrace or anywhere else with your offerings, and welcome all birds as graciously as you would a guest at your dinner table.

THE BLUE TIT

Winter is cruel for many of our smaller native birds. Predators are, of course, a huge factor, but starvation and the cold also pose threats. It is said that only half of tits and a third of blackbirds survive the winter, and most who do are unlikely to make it through a second one. Some smaller birds huddle together on winter nights to save energy, such as wrens, who gang together in a fluffy heap, one on top of the other in disused nests or nooks and crannies. However, the blue tit shivers alone on a branch. It may be time to put out some peanuts and give them a chance.

STARLORE

Orion and Gemini dominate the northern skies in January, and this is when the 'winter triangle' can be seen. It is made up of the stars Betelgeuse (in Orion), Sirius (in Canis Major) and Procyon (in Canis Minor), and the three form a neat and unmistakable equilateral triangle when looking to the south. There is also an unusual meteor shower that can be seen in the first week of January: the Quadrantids, named after a now non-existent constellation, Quadrans Muralis. This shower originates in Boötes, the Herdsman. If you trace a line and follow the 'handle' of the Plough, then continue downwards, you will find the big red star Arcturus, which marks the bottom point of kite-shaped Boötes. The Quadrantids are the debris of an ancient asteroid, and the peak of this shower lasts only a few hours for one night, so you need to check the date online each year to be sure of catching it.

NIGHT SKY REFLECTION

With long nights and short days, the bright stars in January, such as Sirius and Betelgeuse, are reminders that there is always light shining from above, just as there is light shining from within us. On a cloudless night, as you look to the constellations and the stars, try to recall that just as we can call on the moon, we can also draw down the symbolic and magical energy of the celestial canopy. We can use the ancient myths of the stars to help us connect not only to the divine that flows through all things, but also to our ancestors, because we are seeing exactly what they once saw. All in all, this Quiet Moon month is a time for reflecting on the familiar esoteric adage: 'As above, so below.'

TAROT: THE STAR

This card represents the cosmos. It is a card of positive intentions for the month and more to come. Place it on your altar, and maybe light a small white tealight candle beside it as you focus on how you wish your Wicca pathway to proceed in the months ahead. How do you want to work with the Wheel of the Year? And are you aligning yourself more now to ritual and spellwork, or the seasonal energies? Focus on the candle flame, and call on the Earth Goddess and the Sun God to show you the way that is best for you.

The card of inspiration, hope, optimism and blessing, the Star tells you that good things are coming your way, or that you are about to be blessed with peace and harmony as you continue to walk the pathway towards being at one with the divine.

FINAL WORDS

*'If that which thou seekest thou findest not within
thee, thou wilt never find it without thee.'*

DOREEN VALIENTE,
'Charge of the Goddess'

I hope you have enjoyed and will continue to enjoy aligning
yourself with the diverse traditional Wiccan festivities and
celebrations throughout the year. Hopefully, you have also
begun to experience the spirit of Wicca, the central tenet of
which is to be at one with the universe or divine source, and
to experience this mystical nature within yourself.

This book has guided you around the Wheel of the Year
and its seasonal themes, but there is always another season,
another turn of the Wheel, and each time you turn with
these cycles, you can grow and evolve, learning more about
yourself and your place in the cosmos.

Wicca is a diverse belief system that continues to evolve.

We don't have to be part of a coven, but we can if we like. We can join like-minded people for gatherings throughout the year if we have a mind to, or we can practise alone. The divergence of Wicca is such that we can forge our own Wiccan pathways through life. So go gently; you don't have to 'practise' rituals every day or make magic all the time, but you can do so if you like. Or you can just 'be' at one with the world around you. The all-inclusive nature of Wicca is beautifully reflected in the all-inclusive nature of our universe and the divine.

The last line of the Wiccan Rede – 'An ye harm none, do what ye will' – reminds us that all magic must be worked only for positive purposes, and that includes not only for the good of all, but also yourself. And if making magic is about making things happen, then Wicca is where we enable the divine to 'happen upon us'. For the divine that flows through all things also flows through you.

Let the light of the universe shine through you every day. Blessed be.

GLOSSARY

BOOK OF SHADOWS
Similar to a medieval grimoire, this is a book that contains details about spells, ingredients and secret incantations. In the 1940s, Gerald Gardner proposed that covens should keep such a work exclusively for the use of each coven, referring to it as a 'Book of Shadows'. According to Gardner's High Priestess, Doreen Valiente, the name originated from the title of an article in a 1949 edition of the magazine *The Occult Observer*. On one side of a double-page spread there was a mention of Gardner's novel, *High Magic's Aid*, and on the other was an article entitled 'The Book of Shadows', written by well-known palmist Mir Bashir. The article explained how you could foretell a person's future based on the length of their shadow, and Bashir claimed that he had discovered this in an ancient Sanskrit text about divination.

THE FOUR ELEMENTS
The four elements of classical Greek philosophy – fire, earth, air and water – were believed to make up the universe, and

sometimes a fifth element, aether (or spirit in magic belief systems) was also included. Here are their correspondences:

Fire

Fire relates to the colours red, orange and gold, and to red crystals such as red carnelian or ruby. These correspondences enhance and encourage fire qualities within us, such as motivation, leadership, free will and success.

In witchcraft, fire is associated with the cardinal direction south, the sun, the masculine principle, and the Horned God. Witches can also harness the power of fire through working with the suit of wands in Tarot, or with fire's associated zodiac signs, Aries, Leo and Sagittarius. In nature, fire is associated with the landscape, specifically mountains. While in spellwork, fire qualities are encouraged by burning candles or incense, calling on the sun, choosing a time when the luminaries move through a fire sign of the zodiac, or placing a red crystal on one of fire's associated Tarot cards to encourage positive results.

Earth

Earth corresponds to colours such as ochres and brown and earth crystals include smoky quartz, bronzite and mahogany obsidian. These correspondences enhance earth qualities such as tenacity, purpose, stability and concentration.

In witchcraft, earth is associated with the north, and the Earth Goddess. In nature, earth is associated with wildlife, plants, trees, crystals and stones and the earth itself. Witches can use the power of earth through working with the Tarot's suit of pentacles, and with the earth zodiac signs, Taurus,

Virgo and Capricorn. In spellwork earth qualities are enhanced by using herbal, crystal magic or calling on the Earth Goddess, or when the luminaries move through an earth sign of the zodiac.

Air

Air corresponds to colours such as pale and citrine yellows, pastel blues and white. Corresponding crystals include citrine, yellow topaz, blue moss agate, clear quartz crystal.

Air qualities include logic, analysis, objectivity, rational thought, and communication and synthesis of ideas.

In witchcraft, air is associated with the east. Witches can harness the power of air by using the tarot suit of swords, or when the luminaries are moving through the air signs, Gemini, Libra and Aquarius. In nature air is associated with the sky. In spellwork it is associated with wind and sky spirits, and shape-shifting deities or oracles such as Thoth, the Egyptian god of magic, and Morgan le Fey, the sorceress in Arthurian myth.

Water

Water corresponds to colours such as deep blue, light blue, violet, purple and silver. Water's corresponding crystals include amethyst, blue aventurine, moonstone and aquamarine. These crystals encourage intuition, psychic power, spiritual understanding and healing.

In witchcraft, water is associated with the west. Witches can harness the power of water through the suit of cups in Tarot, and the astrological signs Cancer, Scorpio and Pisces. In nature, water is associated with the moon, the tides, and the sea. You can enhance water qualities in your spellwork by calling on lunar goddesses or deities of the darkness and the night.

ECLIPTIC
The apparent pathway of the sun (and all the other planets and the moon as seen from the Earth) as it passes through an imaginary celestial belt encircling the Earth, divided into twelve 30-degree segments, known as the zodiac.

EPHEMERIS
A set of astronomical tables that inform us of at what degree of the ecliptic (see *above*) each of the planets, sun and moon is at for every day of every year, according to certain latitudes. Unless you understand the terms and the symbols associated with the ephemeris, it's easier to look up this information online.

FIXED STARS
Fixed stars are stars visible to the naked eye, which don't appear to move relative to one another in the night sky. Fixed stars make up most of the constellations or can appear alone (such as the North Star, Polaris, which marks the location of the north celestial pole). However, the planets (planet meaning 'a wandering star' in ancient Greek), along with the moon, comets, meteors and satellites, appear to move against the backdrop of the fixed stars and constellations.

NADIR
The lowest point reached by a heavenly body as it appears to travel around another celestial body. In astronomy, this usually refers to the sun or planets when they appear closest to the horizon (the Earth).

SHOOTING STARS
Also known as meteors, these flashes of light streaking across the sky occur when meteoroids (objects in space such as dust grain, space rocks and asteroids) burn up as they enter the Earth's atmosphere.

SYNODIC PERIOD
This is a period of time for a celestial body, such as a planet or the moon, to return to the same or approximately the same position relative to the sun as seen by an observer on the Earth.

ZENITH
The highest point reached by a heavenly body as it appears to travel around another celestial body. In astronomy this refers mostly to the planets or the sun, as they appear to orbit the Earth.

ACKNOWLEDGEMENTS

I want to thank everyone at Piatkus for their support for allowing *The Wiccan Almanac* to come into being. Mostly, thanks to Bernadette Marron for her patience and for keeping me on track! There are so many people involved in publishing a book, and we authors don't often get to meet the whole team, so to all those involved in bringing this book to life, I would like to send you my blessings.

I would also like to thank my family and friends for their love, encouragement and inspiration.

ABOUT THE AUTHOR

Sarah Bartlett is a professional astrologer and illustrator, and author of internationally bestselling books such as *The Little Book of Magic* series, *The Tarot Bible*, *The Secrets of the Universe in 100 Symbols* and the *National Geographic Guide to the World's Supernatural Places*. Sarah lives in the countryside, where she practises natural magic and other esoteric arts.